SIXTH SENSE

TO
BRENDAN & IRINA
WITH
Love & Best Wishes
Positively

The Golden Key to Unlock Your Infinite Potential

SIXTH SENSE

AWAKENED AND EMPOWERED SUBCONSCIOUS MIND

Eugene N. Nwosu

Author of International Bestsellers *Cut Your Own Firewood—the Ultimate Power to Succeed* **and** *Optimal Edge— Unlocking and Enhancing Leadership Potential in People and Organizations*

2017 Eugene N. Nwosu
All rights reserved.

ISBN: 1540627144
ISBN 13: 9781540627148

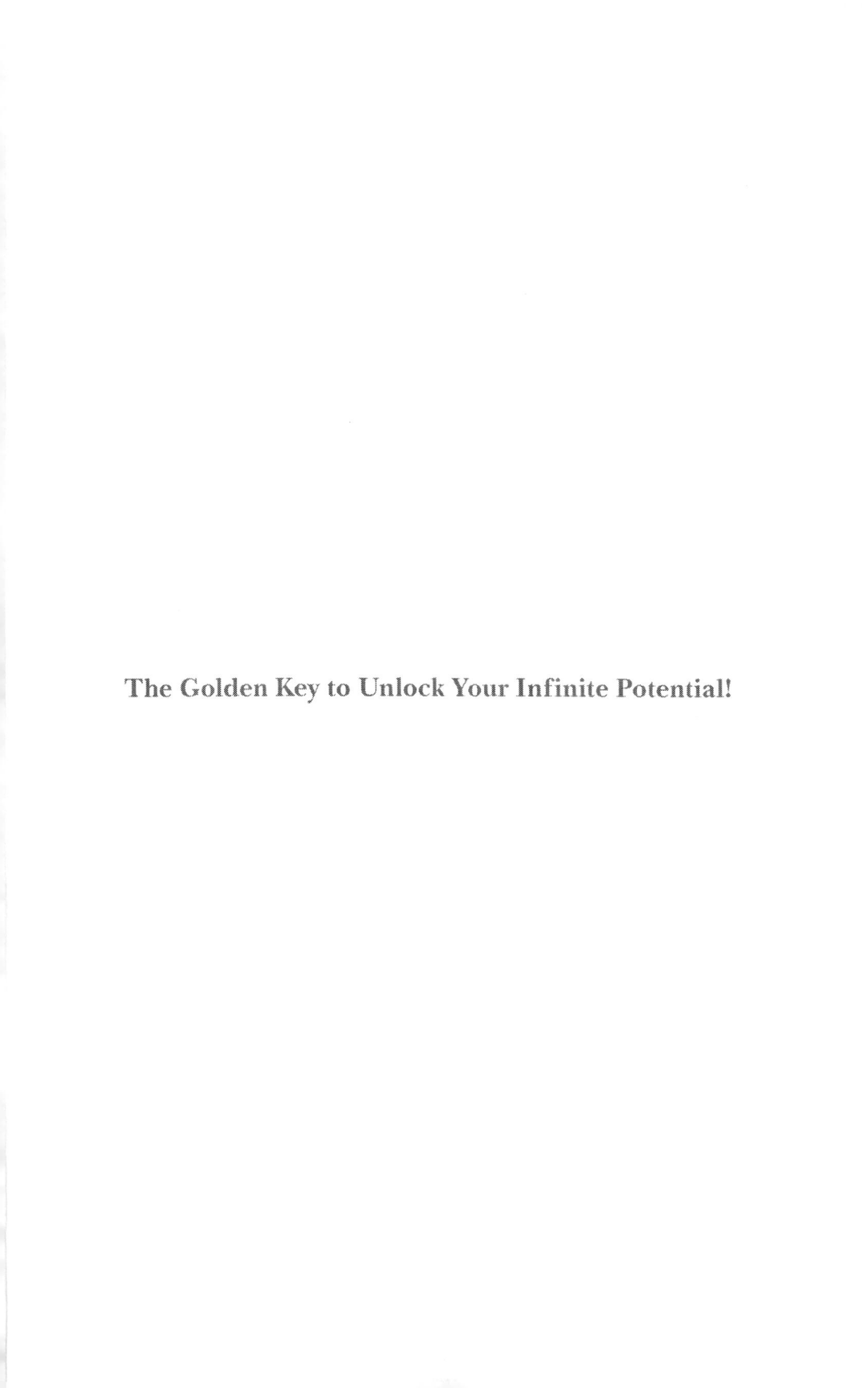

The Golden Key to Unlock Your Infinite Potential!

Believe Your Greatness!

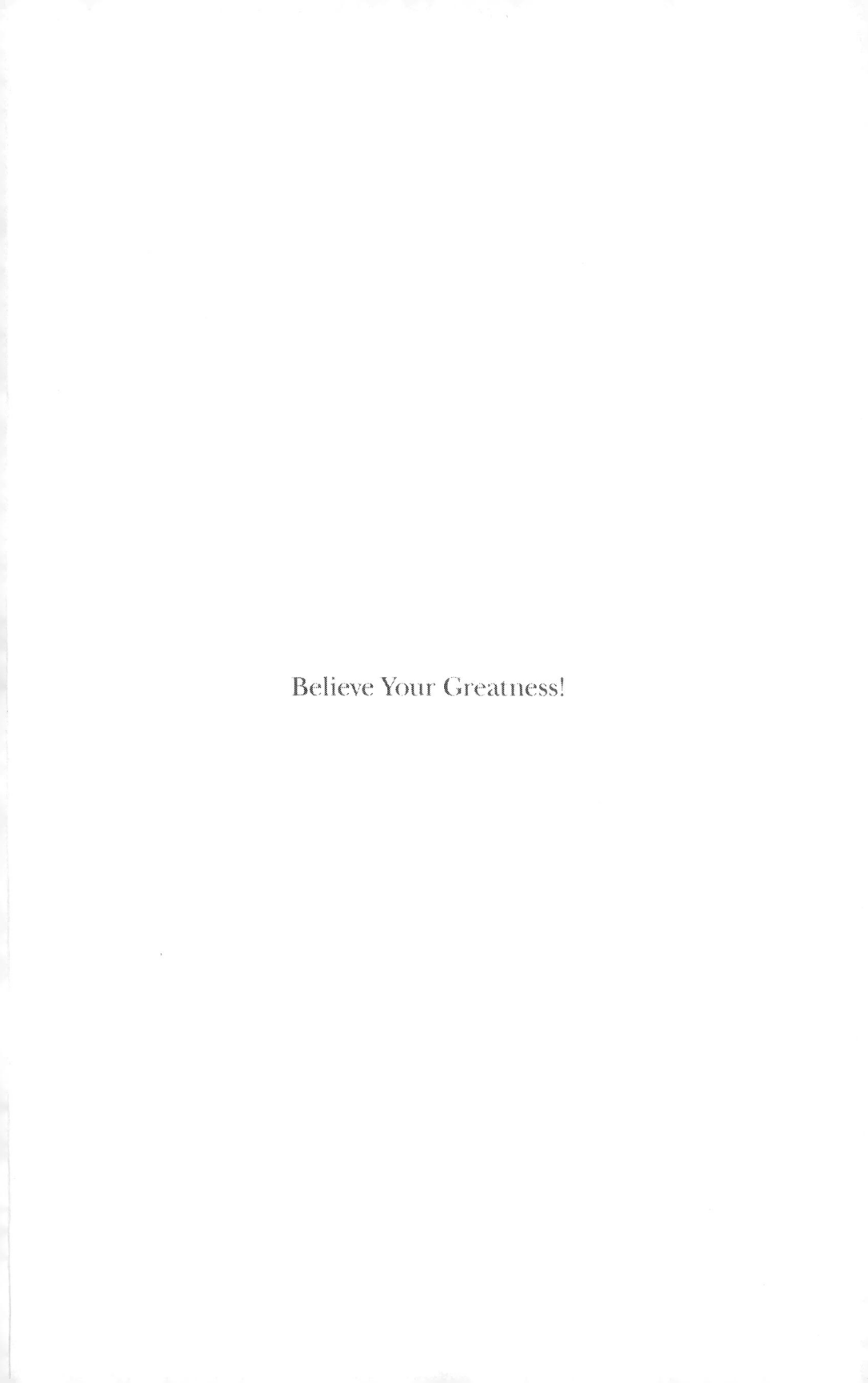

Wisdom allows nothing to be good that will not be so forever; no man to be happy but he that needs no other happiness than what he has within himself; no man to be great or powerful that is not master of himself.

—Lucius Annaeus Seneca

To the expansion of positive, dynamic, and
creative consciousness.
With gratitude, love, and goodwill to all,
always…positively!

CONTENTS

Foreword · xv
Acknowledgments · xvii
Introduction · xxi

Miracle and Magic of the Subconscious Mind · · · · · · · · · · 1
Life's Paradoxes and Enigmas · · · · · · · · · · · · · · · · · · 6
Love—the Most Powerful! · 11
The Simplicity of It All · 15
Wonders of Affirmation! · 18
Warning: This Could Be the Turning Point of Your Life, Positively! · 21
Empowered Belief · 25
Your Infinite Potentials · 31
The Awesome Power of Your Super-Divine-Subconscious Mind · 40
The Wisdom to Succeed · 46
The Potent Power of the "I Am, God Is, We Are One" Paradigm · 53
Two Sides of the Mind · 57
The Conscious and Subconscious Mind at Work · · · · · · · · 60
As You Sow, So Shall You Reap! · · · · · · · · · · · · · · · · · 63
The Wisdom of Responsibility · · · · · · · · · · · · · · · · · · 75

Empowering Question to the Subconscious · · · · · · · · · · ·78
What We Focus upon Expands· · · · · · · · · · · · · · · · · · ·80
Words Have Tremendous Power· · · · · · · · · · · · · · · · ·82
Affirmation Challenge ·87
You Can Do All Things!· ·89
Empowered and Healthy Subconscious Mind · · · · · · · · ·91
Affirmation for Healing and Vibrant Health · · · · · · · · ·96
Empowered and Creative Consciousness · · · · · · · · · · · ·98
Like Attracts Like · 104
Look for the Good!· 107
Nothing Stays the Same· 111
Change Your Subconscious Thoughts—Change
Your Results!· 119
The Two Scopes of the One Mind · · · · · · · · · · · · · · · 126
The Power of Autosuggestion· · · · · · · · · · · · · · · · · · 135
The Outside Forces · 137
Daily Affirmation to Empower the Subconscious Mind · · 146
Think Good Thoughts and Trust Your
Subconscious Mind · 152
The Mightiest Power in Existence· · · · · · · · · · · · · · · 160
Some Guiding Principles for Balance, Equilibrium,
and Equanimity · 166
The Awakened and Empowered Present! · · · · · · · · · · 168
Awaken Your Omnipotent Powers Now! · · · · · · · · · · 174
Your Inside-Out "Book of Life" · · · · · · · · · · · · · · · · 178
Your Subconscious Is in Control Always!· · · · · · · · · · 187
Watch Your Thoughts!· 190
Eugene N. Nwosu · 195

FOREWORD

Our ambition should be to rule ourselves, the true kingdom for each one of us; and true progress is to know more, and be more, and to do more.

—Oscar Wilde

THE PRIMARY MOTIVE of this book is to empower you with the knowledge, tools, and resources that you can use to harness the realm of infinite power of your Super-divine-subconscious mind through effective affirmations to achieve your heart's desires.

The down-to-earth practicality of the affirmation techniques offered in this book is unique. It is presented in simple, easy-to-use formulas, which you can simply apply in your daily life without interruption to your daily activities.

The several ways of planting the seed of positivity in the Super-divine-subconscious mind for definite results as proffered in this book make it particularly useful and incredibly valuable, generally and always, and especially in times of trouble.

The world as you used to know it is about to become clearer and simpler. It is said that "when the student is ready, the teacher will appear." That you have access to this book is an obvious sign that you are ready to take that giant step to trigger, with love and responsibility, the most powerful mechanism of the infinite power of your Super-divine-subconscious mind for greater success. Through the affirmation formulas offered in this book, you will be empowered to achieve your heart's desires, holistically; your paradigm will shift to greater heights. You will start to operate from illuminated, enlightened, and higher consciousness. You will be awakened and empowered to live your life with courage, strong self-control, and strength, and with increased awareness, knowledge, wisdom, and mastery; above all, you will live your life with balance, calmness, and power—onward, upward, and God-ward.

The world is only in the mind of its maker. Do not believe it is outside of yourself.

—Helen Schucman

ACKNOWLEDGMENTS

> Sometimes the first duty of intelligent men is the restatement of the obvious.
>
> —GEORGE ORWELL

I AM DEEPLY grateful to the greatest human beings of all time, the greatest thought masters of all centuries and generations who generously shared their indelible and timeless wisdom that I have been blessed to study and learn from.

> It is not once nor twice but times without number that the same ideas make their appearance in the world.
>
> —ARISTOTLE

Though my life is mine to create, I truly and deeply know and strongly believe that in my own Infinite-devine-Universe, my life is full of abundance; I am grateful, happy, fulfilled, and excited because I am surrounded by people who are eager to contribute to my abundance.

EUGENE N. NWOSU

I am enormously grateful to Lori ..., CreateSpace Editor who, with love and responsibility, helped to fine-tune, refine and transform my raw, straight from-the-heart, divinely inspired, and passionate script into masterpiece.

To my sisters, brothers, cousins, nieces, nephews, inlaws, and all my extended families and esteemed friends, colleagues, and brethren around the world --- you've my gratitude, love, and goodwill, always ... xxx ... Positively!

I am ever so very grateful, happy, fulfilled, and excited because I truly and deeply know and strongly believe that I am a citizen of the world, all human kind are my brethren, to do good is my religion, and every human heart is my church/mosque/synagogue/shrine/temple; because I am, God is, and we are one!

I am grateful and happy to share my unique gifts of creative talent generously with others and to make a meaningful contribution and significant difference to society, positively!

> Borrowing knowledge of reality from all sources, taking the best from every study, science of mind brings together the highest enlightenment of the ages.
>
> —Ernest Holmes

My life is a blissful adventure, one joyful experience after another. I celebrate love, life, and abundance every day. My love of life is positively infectious. I bless my life every day. I see the good in every situation, and I see beauty everywhere. I see miracles everywhere, and the more joyful and happy thoughts I generate, the more magical my life becomes.

> When you meet anyone, remember it is a holy encounter. As you see him, you will see yourself…for in him you will find yourself or lose yourself.
>
> —Helen Schucman

The magic, miracle, and essence of the infinite, divine, universal energy and God's love is made manifest in my life through the nearest and dearest human beings around me, my immediate family.

To Ursula, Gus, Poppy, Ozi, and Ima Nwosu, and all the lovely children who, over the years, accorded me the privilege, honour, pleasure, joy and happiness of being your husband, father, foster parent, and legal guardian; I am indeed grateful for the experience of having all of you in my immediate household—having all of you in my life is one of the most loving and experientially challenging, spiritually uplifting, and humbling responsibilities of my life. I am ever so very grateful, joyful, and happy for the immense and immeasurable contribution you make in my exciting and fulfilling experiential life.

EUGENE N. NWOSU

> I believe in living a poetic life, an art full life. Everything we do from the way we raise our children to the way we welcome our friends is part of a large canvas we are creating.
>
> —Maya Angelou

INTRODUCTION

I know of no more encouraging fact than the unquestionable ability of man to elevate his life by conscious endeavor.

—HENRY DAVID THOREAU

YOU MUST CHANGE the inner conditions of the mind if you wish to change your external conditions. Most people spend a lifetime of energy and resources trying to change circumstances and conditions by working on the circumstances and conditions that created the situations. They fail to see the connection. They fail to understand that all circumstances and conditions emanate from causes. They don't realize that their conditions flow from a cause.

To eliminate disharmony, strife, disorder, poverty, constraints, and limitations in your life, you must eliminate the cause. The way and manner you allow your conscious mind to operate and the thought processes and images you allow in your conscious mind are the cause. Simply put, when you change the cause, the effect will change. If you want more joy and happiness, wealth and prosperity, peace and balance, calmness and tranquility, and power to overcome challenges and achieve unique success, then the greater part of your life must be an inside job (inside out).

> Corrective learning begins with the awakening of spirit and the turning away from belief in physical sight.
>
> —Helen Schucman

You can reprogram and redirect your conscious and subconscious mind to positively shape your environment for better. You will achieve vibrant health; nurture a great and healthy family; have fulfilling and nourishing relationships, a healthy lifestyle, joy and happiness, balance, equilibrium, and calmness; and gain strength, mastery, and the power to triumph in all areas of your life.

If you effectively harness and apply the affirmations offered in this book with an open mind, you will experience wonderful successes in all areas of your life.

You are responsible for most of your past and present successes and limitations because of the conditions of your thought. Whatever you thought, said to yourself, and believed were what formed your perceptions, which turned out to be your reality. All along you have been responsible for the world you live in.

Your awakening and empowering moment begins the moment you accept responsibility for your past and present situation.

SIXTH SENSE

We live in a very orderly, precise, and dynamic universe, and we succeed or fail in proportion to our adherence to the laws of the Infinite-divine-Universe.

When you become passionately engaged in the life and work of your dreams, in alignment with the Infinite-divine-Universal laws, you will succeed all the time.

The laws of the Infinite-divine-Universe are constantly working, whether you know it and whether they seem fair. They operate whether you know about them or use them consciously, so you might as well take hold of them and put them to work for you to deliberately and positively steer and direct your career, relationships, health, spirituality, and finances toward greater good.

Success is a never-ending journey; it is not a specific destination. It is a process that mostly depends on the direction of your choice. It is your progressive journey toward your highest purpose, based on your vision, dreams, and desires in all areas of your life.

> Every choice you make establishes your own identity as you will see it and believe it is.
>
> —HELEN SCHUCMAN

Everything in the Infinite-divine-Universe is energy and all connected. Every thought and feeling creates a vibration, an impulse of energy that goes out into the Infinite-divine-Universe and stays there forever. That is why we attract the things we focus on, think about, and give energy to.

We are spiritual beings in human bodies, and the physical world we experience is only a small part of our true existence. To become successful and stay successful, we must stay connected with the source of all success.

Your subconscious mind is the root of your habits. Everything that happened to you happened because of thoughts impressed on your subconscious mind through your conscious perception and belief.

Change your subconscious thoughts and your life positively for greater good. When you change your subconscious thoughts, you will change your results. If you acknowledge and appreciate this simple principle, with open mind and in good faith, and strongly believe in the infinite powers of your Super-divine-subconscious mind, you will change your life beyond your comprehension and for greater good, and you will achieve worthy and extraordinary successes.

To change your life for greater good, you must design and equip your subconscious mind with positive and empowering seeds. The infinite intelligence of your Super-divine-subconscious mind will be accordingly and appropriately guided and directed to provide you with all the health, wealth, and prosperity for your spiritual, mental, and physical well being.

SIXTH SENSE

The infinite intelligence of your Super-divine-subconscious mind, your sixth sense, can give you independence of time and space. It can make you free of all pain and suffering. It can give you the answer to all problems, whatever they may be. Your sixth sense is a power and an intelligence within you that far transcends your intellect, causing you to marvel at the wonder of it all. When you awaken, and empower the infinite intelligence of your Super-divine-subconscious mind, your sixth sense, you will be excited and joyful at the miracle-working powers latent in your own subconscious mind.

EUGENE N. NWOSU

> If one advances confidently in the direction of his dreams and endeavours to live the life which he has imagined, he will meet with a success unexpected in common hours. He will put some things behind, will pass an invisible boundary; new, universal, and more liberal laws will begin to establish themselves around and within him; or the old laws be expanded, and interpreted in his favour in a more liberal sense, and he will live with the license of a higher order of beings.
>
> —Henry David Thoreau

MIRACLE AND MAGIC OF THE SUBCONSCIOUS MIND

> There are two ways to live: you can live as if nothing is a miracle; you can live as if everything is a miracle.
>
> —Albert Einstein

LIFE AND LIVING can be a miracle or a curse. The choice is always yours to make. Your consciousness is what is at play all the time—choosing, determining, processing, accepting, and rejecting; loving, hating, giving, taking, receiving, creating, building, destroying—these and every other thing in this divine universe, including the ideas of heaven and earth, good and evil, God and devil, and life and death, are made manifest by our conscious mind.

> The strongest principle of growth lies in the human choice.
>
> —George Eliot

EUGENE N. NWOSU

> So divinely is the world organized that every one of us, in our place and time, is in balance with everything else.
>
> —Johann Wolfgang von Goethe

Whatever your conscious mind thinks and believes about any of these and every other of life's events only makes it so, for real!

> Magic is believing in yourself; if you can do that, you can make anything happen.
>
> —Johann Wolfgang von Goethe

The universe and everything in it is pure and unadulterated energy. Everything is energy. The air we breathe; the ground we stand on; the mountains, ocean, and sea; the iron and machines; the human body and ashes; the trees, leaves, and grass—all are pure and unadulterated energy and are connected.

> From wonder into wonder existence opens.
>
> —Lao Tzu

Universal energy is continuously bubbling, buzzing, spinning, and infinitely evolving and unraveling with fathomless, fantastic, and incredible mysteries. The awesomeness and wholesomeness of the universal energy is, in its entirety, a miracle!

SIXTH SENSE

> Miracles, in the sense of phenomena we cannot
> explain, surround us on every hand: life itself is
> the miracle of miracles.
>
> —GEORGE BERNARD SHAW

Phenomenal miracles of extraordinary varieties and mystical dimensions are happening constantly in our world and to men and women in all walks of life all over the world.

> All change is a miracle to contemplate, but it is
> a miracle which is taking place every instant.
>
> —HENRY DAVID THOREAU

Miracles will happen to you too—with mastery and illuminated and enlightened consciousness. You will be able to harness and apply the magic power of your Super-Divine-Subconscious mind and conscientiously and consistently draw from it to grasp and embrace the abundant possibilities and opportunities that are prevalent in this omnipotent and omnipresent universe for greater good in every situation. You will achieve a life of balance, equilibrium, equanimity, and greater success in all areas.

> A man is literally what he thinks, his character
> being the complete sum of all his thoughts.
>
> —JAMES ALLEN, *AS A MAN THINKETH*

Your habitual thinking, perception, and imagery shape, create, and determine your destiny, per James Allen's age-old and timeless discourse, "As a man thinketh, so he is; as he continues to think, so he remains."

> You are the universe; you aren't in the universe.
>
> —Eckhart Tolle

SIXTH SENSE

What a man thinks of himself, that it is which determines, or rather indicates, his fate.

—Henry David Thoreau

Our destiny is not mapped out for us by some exterior power; we map it out for ourselves. What we think and do in the present determines what shall happen to us in the future.

—Christian D. Larson

LIFE'S PARADOXES AND ENIGMAS

Every person is what he is because of his method of thinking, and men and nations differ from each other only because they think differently.

—Charles Francis Haanel

Let's for a moment contemplate and attempt to unravel some of life's dichotomies and conundrums:

- Why are some people joyful and happy and other people sad and unhappy?
- Why are some people peaceful and prosperous and other people deprived, poor, wretched, and miserable?
- Why are some countries developed, organised, peaceful, and progressive and others undeveloped, chaotic, and dangerous to live in?
- Why are some people fearful, nervous, and anxious and others in similar circumstances full of faith, strong self-belief, and self-confidence?

SIXTH SENSE

- Why do some people have beautiful, luxurious homes in lovely and safe environments and others live out a measly existence in slum, shantytown, ghetto environments?
- Why do some people have great and abundant accomplishments and successes and others are abject and hopeless failures?
- Why is one person healed of a so-called incurable disease and another isn't?
- Why do so many good, kind-hearted, religious people suffer tortures on the mind and body and many immoral and nonreligious people succeed, prosper, and enjoy radiant health and long lifes?
- Why is one person happily married and another unmarried, unhappy, and frustrated?

The answer to these poignant issues and questions certainly lies in the simple workings of the conscious and subconscious mind.

> *Nature magically suits a man to his fortunes, by making them the fruit of his character.*
>
> —Ralph Waldo Emerson

EUGENE N. NWOSU

We are what we think. All that we are arises with our thoughts. With our thoughts, we make the world.

—Buddha

SIXTH SENSE

Man, is made or unmade by himself; in the armoury of thought he forges the weapons by which he destroys himself; he also fashions the tools with which he builds for himself heavenly mansions of joy and strength and peace. By the right choice and true application of thought, man ascends to the Divine Perfection; by the abuse and wrong application of thought, he descends below the level of the beast. Between these two extremes are all the grades of character, and man is their maker and master.

—JAMES ALLEN, *As a Man Thinketh*

EUGENE N. NWOSU

I am love! You are love! God is love! We are one with God's love!

--- EUGENE N. NWOSU

LOVE–THE MOST POWERFUL!

We are born of love; love is our mother.

—Rumi

Love is of all passions the strongest, for it attacks simultaneously the head, the heart, and the senses.

—Lao Tzu

LOVE IS THE most powerful and positive creative force that can lift you up from confusion, misery, depression, and failure, and unlock your potential, solve your difficulties, release you from emotional and physical bondage, and place you on the majestic road to freedom, joy, and peace of mind.

If you could only love enough, you could be the most powerful person in the world.

—Emmet Fox

> He who is in love is wise and is becoming wiser,
> sees newly every time he looks at the object
> beloved, drawing from it with his eyes and his
> mind those virtues which it possesses.
>
> —Ralph Waldo Emerson

Love is the pure essence that propels and empowers the miracle working powers of your subconscious mind to heal any sickness and make vital organs strong again.

> Love does not dominate; it cultivates.
>
> —Johann Wolfgang von Goethe

When you learn, and understand how to harness and apply the inner workings of your Super-divine-subconscious mind with love and responsibility, you will break free from fear and enter the glorious liberty of self-control and strength, increased awareness, knowledge, wisdom, mastery, and ultimate calmness and power.

> Love is a state of being. Your love is not outside;
> it is deep within you. You can never lose it, and
> it cannot leave you. It is not dependent on some
> other body, some external form.
>
> —Eckhart Tolle

SIXTH SENSE

There is no difficulty that enough love will not conquer, no disease that enough love will not heal; no door that enough love will not open; no gulf that enough love will not bridge; no wall that enough love will not throw down; no sin that enough love will not redeem…it makes no difference how deeply seated may be the trouble; how hopeless the outlook; how muddled the tangle; how great the mistake. A sufficient realization of love will dissolve it all. If only you could love enough you would be the happiest and most powerful being in the world.

—Emmet Fox

There is no remedy for love, but to love more.

—Henry David Thoreau

Through love all that is bitter will be sweet, through love all that is copper will be gold, through love all dregs will become wine, through love all pain will turn to medicine.

—Rumi

EUGENE N. NWOSU

It is easy to hate and it is difficult to love. This is how the whole scheme of things works. All good things are difficult to achieve, and bad things are very easy to get.

—Confucius

A loving heart is the truest wisdom.

—Charles Dickens

THE SIMPLICITY OF IT ALL

The road to freedom lies not through mysteries or occult performances, but through the intelligent use of natural forces and laws.

—Ernest Holmes

Life is made up of two kinds of elements—positives and negatives. Our lives revolve around these natural forces, whether joy, happiness, career, health, money, or relationships. Whether we have good or bad times, good or bad days, good or bad months, good or bad years. Whether we are filled with joy and happiness or sadness and unhappiness. Whether our work, business, or career is exciting, satisfying, and flourishing or unfulfilling and unrewarding. Whether we are rich or poor, with plenty of money or lack of money.

Life is a mirror and will reflect, back to the thinker what he thinks into it.

—Ernest Holmes

Whenever there are more negative occurrences than positive in our lives, we know something is not particularly right. There are people you know whose lives are filled with wonderful things; they are constantly joyful, happy, and fulfilled, and at the back of your mind, you know that you too deserve similar blessings. Yes! We all deserve lives of joy and happiness, wealth and prosperity, vibrant health and healthy lifestyle, and balance, equilibrium, and equanimity.

> Human beings can alter their lives by altering their attitudes of mind.
>
> —William James

Remarkably, a lot of people who are blessed and enjoy these wonderful things may not know exactly how to explain what it was that they did or how they got it. One thing is for sure: they unconsciously harnessed and applied the greatest and most powerful positive force of the universe—love—that is the cause of all goodness.

SIXTH SENSE

> Without exception, every person who has a great life used love to achieve it. The power to have all the positive and good things in life is love!
>
> —Ronda Byrne

WONDERS OF AFFIRMATION!

By believing passionately in something that does not yet exist, we create it. The nonexistent is whatever we have not sufficiently desired.

—Nikos Kazantzakis

AFFIRMATION IS THE harmonious interaction of the conscious and subconscious mind, purposefully and specifically directed toward a desired objective. Wonderful things can happen when your conscious and subconscious interact harmoniously and effectively. This book contains the fundamental principles, formulas, tools, and guides to help awaken and empower you with the knowledge and wisdom to harness and utilize the realm of infinite power of your Super-divine-subconscious mind through effective and specifically directed affirmations to achieve your heart's disires.

SIXTH SENSE

> Every mental process, or every mental action, that takes place in our wide-awake consciousness will, if it has depth of feeling or intensity, enter the unconscious field, and after it has developed itself per the line of its original nature, will return to the conscious side of the mind.
>
> —Christian D. Larson

You deserve a more joyful, happier, richer, fulfilling, and exciting life. When you learn the simple methods of harnessing and using your Super-divine-subconscious mind, you will break the chains of negativity and usher in positivity, balance, harmony, and smoothness in your relationships and in your daily affairs and solve business and career issues without stress.

EUGENE N. NWOSU

> Whatever you habitually think yourself to be, that you are. You must form, now, a greater and better habit; you must form a conception of yourself as a being of limitless power and habitually think that you are that being. It is the habitual, not the periodical, thought that decides your destiny.
>
> —Wallace D. Wattles

WARNING: THIS COULD BE THE TURNING POINT OF YOUR LIFE, POSITIVELY!

I TRULY KNOW and strongly believe if you read and apply the several affirmation exercises and techniques in this book, earnestly and with an open mind—just to prove to yourself the wonderful ways it can holistically transform your consciousness and your life—it could be the most sensational turning point and the beginning of the greatest journey of your life.

> Genius at first is little more than a great capacity for receiving discipline.
>
> —GEORGE ELLIOT

You will be opened to the inner workings and become aware of the awesome powers of your Super-divine-subconscious mind. You will understand and appreciate your unique and dynamic place; comprehend your holistic part in the affairs; and begin to take seriously your creative responsibility in the ever evolving and changing Infinite-divine-Universe. You will begin to seriously hold yourself accountable for your past and present and accordingly and appropriately start to take active and direct responsibility for the shaping of your tomorrow, today!

> Imagination is the beginning of creation. You imagine what you desire, you will what you imagine, and at last you create what you will.
>
> —George Bernard Shaw

The down-to-earth practicality of the affirmation techniques offered in this book is unique. It is presented in simple, easy-to-use formulas, which you can apply in your daily life without interruption to your activities.

> The power for creating a better future is contained in the present moment: you create a good future by creating a good present.
>
> —Eckhart Tolle

People don't think and act reasonably in times of trouble, and they need an obviously easy pattern and workable formula to follow. This book will give you colossal advantage, particularly in time of difficulty, because of the numerous easy-to-apply formulas and tools which you can harness and utilize to re-wire, re-direct, and plant seeds of positivity in the Super-divine-subconscious mind -- Sixth Sense; being the engine, store-house, and main source and realm of your infinite potentials and possibilities, for definite results and successes in all things, positively!

> Intense desire, therefore, is the first requisite in becoming a Master Mind. Those who have made a mark in this world—those who have ascended to the heights—are those who desired intensely and incessantly. Those weak in desire never reach Mastery or the Heights until they become strong and soulfully passionate in desire.
>
> —CHARLES FRANCIS HAANEL

> Realize deeply that the present moment is all you ever have. Make the Now the primary focus of your life.
>
> —Eckhart Tolle

> Use the imagination to picture only what is good, what is beautiful, what is beneficial, what is ideal, and what you wish to realize. Mentally see yourself receiving what you deeply desire to receive. What you imagine, you will think, and what you think, you will become. Therefore, if you imagine only those things that are in harmony with what you wish to obtain or achieve, all your thinking will soon tend to produce what you want to attain or achieve.
>
> —Christian D. Larson

EMPOWERED BELIEF

> What a man believes may be ascertained, not from his creed, but from the assumptions on which he habitually acts.
>
> —GEORGE BERNARD SHAW

WARNING! WHATEVER YOUR belief might be is about to change. Your entire life will equally change, positively and for greater good. A paradigm shift of extraordinary magnitude is about to happen to you, positively! You are about to become subliminally illuminated and enlightened beyond measure about the world around you and your special, unique, and powerful connection to it all. With an open-mind and a little commitment, you will learn how to script your own awesome template for living; and no longer depend on abstract motivational techniques and methods that lead you a little further until it wears-off. You will learn how to plant the right and appropriate seeds for your deserved bountiful harvest. You will learn and gain the all-important wisdom about how to string-together your own fishing rod and regularly obtain fish to feed; rather than depend on the intermittent fish handed out by middle-men and third-parties via inspirational and motivational abstracts that only last you, a while. That you have possession of this book is no accident or happen's-chance. You are ready to take that giant step toward self-awareness, self-realisation, self-control and strenght, empowering wisdom and mastery, and overall calmness and power. The world as you used to know is about to become extraordinarily clearer and simpler.

> Nothing splendid has ever been achieved except by those who dared believe that something inside them was superior to circumstance.
>
> —Bruce Barton

You are ready to begin the sowing of the elemental seeds of success, which you shall harvest and reap the deserved rewards, positively, in all areas of your life. You are ready to start the process of harnessing and applying the infinite power of your Super-divine-subconscious mind for greater good and holistic success and to achieve balance, equilibrium, and equanimity.

> Some look at things that are and ask why. I dream of things that never were and ask why not?
>
> —George Bernard Shaw

SIXTH SENSE

I have learned through several decades of studying and partaking in religious and spiritual faiths and doctrines and lifelong research and personal experiences tha it is not particularly the thing believed in that brings an answer to one's prayer; the answer to prayer occurs when the individual's subconscious mind is in alignment with the mental picture or thought in his or her mind.

> Dogmas are collective conceptual prisons. And the strange thing is that people love their prison cells because they give them a sense of security and a false sense of "I know." Nothing has inflicted more suffering on humanity than its dogmas.
>
> —ECKHART TOLLE

The miracle-working power of the infinite Super-divine-subconscious mind is part of the omnipotent and omnipresent universal energy. It predates human beings—it existed before you were born and before any church, mosque, temple, synagogue, or world existed. The great eternal truths and principles of life predate all faiths and religions.

> God is the universal substance in existing things. "It" comprises all things. "It" is the fountain of all being. In "it" exists everything that is.
>
> —LUCIUS ANNAEUS SENECA

It is with these facts that I encourage you to study and grasp the very life-changing information in this book. You can apply the affirmation techniques to awaken and empower the transformative power of your infinite Super-divine-subconscious mind to minimize strife and suffering, heal mental and physical wounds, and prevent poverty, failure, misery, and frustration.

Start today to let wonders happen in your life! All you must do is unite mentally and emotionally with the good you wish to embody, with love and responsibility, and the creative powers of your Super-divine-subconscious mind will respond accordingly.

> Let a man radically alter his thoughts, and he will be astonished at the rapid transformation effect it will have in the material conditions of his life.
>
> —JAMES ALLEN, *As a Man Thinketh*

SIXTH SENSE

> Here is how you can awaken the infinite intelligence of the Super-divine-subconscious mind, your sixth sense, to be reborn and empowered: get still and quiet by relaxing the mind and body. Detach yourself from the old way of thinking and form a new concept of yourself, a new estimate. Meditate on the reality of this new concept to the point of conviction. Envision and feel the reality of the new ideal; live with it; envelop it in love; woo it; then the ideal will be resurrected in you, and you will become a changed person.
>
> —Eugene N. Nwosu

There is one mind common to all regardless of one's religious affiliation. All religions of the world can attest to the law of belief as the most important factor responsible for the answer to prayers. The answer to prayer happens when the subconscious mind responds to the mental picture or thought in the individual's mind. This is psychologically true with all religions. The law of belief is the law of life, and belief could simply be described as a thought in your mind. As a man thinks, feels, and believes, so is the condition of his mind, body, and circumstances.

> Belief creates the "actual" fact.
>
> —William James

The law of belief is operating in all religions of the world, and everyone gets answers to their prayers with a strong sense of belief, whether you are Buddhist, Christian, Muslim, Jewish, pagan, atheist, or nonaligned freethinker. Basically, answered prayer is the realization of your subconscious desire.

> Man, is made by his belief. As he believes, so he is.
>
> —Johann Wolfgang von Goethe

Everyone may get answers to their prayers, not because of the creed, religion, affiliation, ritual, ceremony, formula, liturgy, spiritual exercises, incantation, sacrifices, or offerings, but solely because of the strong subconscious belief or mental alignment and acceptance about that for which the person has prayed.

YOUR INFINITE POTENTIALS

*For a man to achieve all that is demanded of him,
he must regard himself as greater than he is.*

—Johann Wolfgang von Goethe

Within your Super-divine-subconscious mind lies infinite potential of incredible magnitude. You possess within you boundless and immeasurable power and riches. These unlimited potentials you are blessed with are always within your reach. All you must do to gain them is just open your mind with love and embrace them. The infinite power of the universe and the possibilities it offers have always been here available, limitless, and yours for using any time. To gain them, all you must do is have an open mind to embrace the infinite possibilities within you.

That is the real spiritual awakening, when something emerges from within you that is deeper than who you thought you were. So, the person is still there, but one could almost say that something more powerful shines through the person.

—Eckhart Tolle

SIXTH SENSE

There is within you the omnipotent, omnipresent, omniscient, divine ocean of love and mercy, like a storehouse with infinite and abundant riches, which you can draw from to meet all your needs.

> As soon as you trust yourself, you will know
> how to live.
>
> —Johann Wolfgang von Goethe

Don't be like many people who are closed off to their own potential because they do not know about this storehouse of infinite intelligence and boundless ocean of love and mercy within themselves. You know now that whatever you want, you can draw it forth.

> In everything, depend upon yourself, but work in harmony with all things. Do not depend even upon the Infinite, but learn to work and live in harmony with the Infinite. The highest teachings of the Christ reveal most clearly the principle that no soul was created to be a mere helpless instrument in the hands of Supreme Power, but that every soul should act and live in perfect oneness with that Power. And the promise is that we all are not only to do the things that Christ did, but even greater things.
>
> —Christian D. Larson

We know that a magnetized piece of iron will lift more than a dozen times its own weight. But when this same piece of iron is demagnetized, it will not be able to lift even a feather. Relatively, two types of people exist in the world. The first are the ones who are magnetic with self-esteem, self-confidence, strong faith, positive outlook, winning mentality, and success.

> The will to win, the desire to succeed, the urge to reach your full potential…these are the keys that will unlock the door to personal excellence.
>
> —Confucius

SIXTH SENSE

The second type of people are the ones who dwell on negativity most of the time. They are like the demagnetized piece of metal. They are so pessimistic, full of doubts, and fearful most of the time. People in this category never make it far enough in life. Pessimism, fear, and doubt always hold them down and stop them from moving far forward.

> People tend to dwell more on negative things than on good things. So, the mind then becomes obsessed with negative things, with judgments, guilt, and anxiety produced by thoughts about the future and so on.
>
> —Eckhart Tolle

The principles in this book will fundamentally help you become magnetic, and through the affirmation formulas, tools, and techniques, you will be empowered to holistically achieve your heart's desires. With gratitude, love, and responsibility, you shall have absolute control over the entire events in your life. You will have the authority and power through your infinite Super-divine-subconscious mind to design, create, and enjoy vibrant health; be a proud parent of a great and healthy family; and become financially free and independent. Joy, happiness, and peace of mind shall be yours, and you will overflow with gratitude, love, and goodwill, which you can extend to all.

EUGENE N. NWOSU

> There is no passion to be found playing small—
> in settling for a life that is less than the one you
> are capable of living.
>
> —Nelson Mandela

Yes! When you comprehend, and recognize your unique place in this Infinite-divine-Universe, how very important you are, how the universe and everything about it is pure energy, how you are part and parcel of everything about the universe, how you are part and parcel of the omnipresent and omnipotent universal energy, then you can authoritatively believe that nothing in the universe is beyond you. You have equal access to everything in the universe, and all its wealth and possibilities are available for you.

There is no limit to anything in the world. There's more than enough of everything for everyone in the world. You can now go ahead and strongly believe that you are one with the Infinite-divine energy of the universe.

> Everything is the product of one universal
> creative effort. There is nothing dead in
> Nature. Everything is organic and living, and
> therefore the whole world appears to be a living
> organism.
>
> —Lucius Annaeus Seneca

SIXTH SENSE

The Infinite-divine-Universe is pure love-energy—God! Everything, including human beings, is energy, and all is connected. Everything is connected to the Infinite-divine-Universal energy, that being pure love-energy, God. You and everyone and everything are connected to the one and only pure love-energy, God. You and everyone are one with God, and God is connected to everything; therefore, we are one!

> Everything that happens, happens, as it should, and if you observe carefully, you will find this to be so.
>
> —Marcus Aurelius

The first and most potent and empowering affirmation being offered here will illuminate and ease your mind, bring you peace, guide you, save you from unforeseen danger, protect you from harm, smoothen your day, open your intuitive mind, and help you achieve balance, equilibrium, and equanimity.

> Make the pattern clear, and make it beautiful; do not be afraid—make it grand. Remember that no limitation can be placed upon you by anyone but yourself; you are not limited as to cost or material; draw on the Infinite for your supply, construct it in your imagination; it must be there before it will ever appear anywhere else.
>
> —Charles Francis Haanel

Here are some simple affirmations you can apply anytime to powerfully transform your life for greater good:

> I am ever so very grateful. I am ever so very happy. I am ever so much fulfilled. I am ever so very excited now that I truly and deeply know and strongly believe that in my own Infinite-divine-Universe, I am love, I am responsible, I am accountable, I am powerful, I am a winner, I am winning, I am financially independent, I am financially free, I am financially successful, I am healthy, I am wealthy, I am rich, I am prosperous, and I truly and deeply know and strongly believe that I am worthy of all my desires because I am, God is, and we are one!

OK! These few words of affirmation are so simple, and I urge you to give it a try with an open mind. One thing is for sure: there is no special ritual to it, no kneeling down and reciting it, no special privacy or sitting quietly for minutes or hours for results. You can easily learn these few words within the blink of an eye. All you need to do is embrace these words with an open mind and repeat them to yourself, quietly or verbally, while you are carrying out any of your normal activities, such as in the shower or cooking.

SIXTH SENSE

> As a single footstep, will not make a path on the earth, so a single thought will not make a pathway in the mind. To make a deep physical path, we walk again and again. To make a deep mental path, we must think over and over the kind of thoughts we wish to dominate our lives.
>
> —HENRY DAVID THOREAU

Spend at least seven days practicing, repeating, and contemplating these affirmations, and watch and observe the difference in your behavior and the changes in situations and circumstances around you. One thing is for sure: your conscious mind will be opened to better understand your past, present, and future. You will have improved, illuminated, and enlightened awareness and better self-control and strength to manage your affairs. Your knowledge and mastery of your situation will improve, and you shall have the calmness and power of self-belief, self-confidence, and self-esteem.

THE AWESOME POWER OF YOUR SUPER-DIVINE-SUBCONSCIOUS MIND

> The purpose of life for man is growth...
> man can grow as he will...man can develop
> any power which is or has been shown by any
> person anywhere. Nothing that is possible in
> spirit is impossible in flesh and blood. Nothing
> that man can think is impossible. Nothing that
> man can imagine is impossible of realization.
>
> —WALLACE D. WATTLES

THERE LIES WITHIN every man and woman the greatest power of the Super-divine-subconscious mind. It is the miracle-creative power that is at work in this Infinite-divine-Universe, and once you learn and understand how to harness and use the infinite power of your Super-divine-subconscious mind, you can attract to yourself all that you desire and deserve, be it more wealth, vibrant health, a healthy and loving family, joy and happiness, and healthy lifestyle.

SIXTH SENSE

> *Every person above the ordinary has a certain mission that they are called to fulfill.*
>
> —Johann Wolfgang von Goethe

Fortunately, you do not need to look elsewhere for this Infinite-Super-divine power. It's already in you. You were born with it. It is that pure essence in you—infinite, divine, and pure. It is the pure love-energy, the soul, that you were born with. Your soul is divine, pure, and unadulterated God's love. Soul is part and parcel of the universal energy, and the universe and everything in it is energy, or God's love. You already possess it. But you must learn how to properly harness and use it for greater good. You must understand how to use it for greater benefit in all areas of your life.

> *Everyone has been made for some particular work, and the desire for that work has been put in every heart.*
>
> —Rumi

Choose now to create a much more wonderful, effective, wealthy, prosperous, and dignified life than ever before. The simple procedures and methods described in this book will help you gain the essential knowledge, understanding, and enlightenment that will enable you to realize your heart's desires and make your hopes and dreams come true.

> There is a world within—a world of thought and feeling and power; of light and life and beauty; and, although invisible, its forces are mighty.
>
> —Charles Francis Haanel

You know now that you possess within your infinite Super-divine-subconscious mind immeasurable wisdom, infinite power, and an infinite supply of all that is necessary to achieve all you desire and deserve. It is waiting there for you to harness and use. Start now to acknowledge and appreciate the infinite potentialities of your Super-divine-subconscious mind to manifest all you need for joy and happiness, peace and tranquility, and to live a healthier and fruitful life.

Once more, I ask that you maintain an open mind, for if you keep an open mind and remain receptive, the infinite intelligence of your Super-divine-subconscious mind will disclose to you all that you need to know at every moment, at the appropriate time and space. You will be able to generate new thoughts and ideas, create new works of art, produce invention, make new discoveries, and cause several unimaginable events to happen for your greater good. The infinite intelligence in your Super-divine-subconscious mind can give you access to extraordinary new kinds of knowledge. Allow your

SIXTH SENSE

Super-divine-subconscious mind to open and bestow its wonderful powers to you, and your life will change and be catapulted to greater heights, positively!

> Since new developments are the products of a creative mind, we must therefore stimulate and encourage that type of mind in every way possible.
>
> —George Washington Carver

Through the awesome power of your Super-divine-subconscious mind, you can attract the ideal companion, as well as the right business associate or partner. The infinite power of your Super-divine-subconscious mind will show you how to attract all the wealth you deserve and lead you to the ways and means to achieve financial independence and freedom and all your heart's desires.

> What lies behind us and what lies ahead of us are tiny matters compared to what lives within us.
>
> —Henry David Thoreau

Within your Super-divine-subconscious mind lies the solution for every problem and the cause for every effect. You have the divine right to discover this inner world of thought, feeling, and power, of light, love, and beauty that are latent in you. It is the mightiest force in the universe. When you learn how to trigger this incredible positive force of love and can harness and tap from its wonderful powers, you will acquire the most potent and powerful wisdom necessary to create and live a life of balance, abundance, security, gratitude, joy, happiness, equanimity, and power.

SIXTH SENSE

Wisdom is the essential basis of greatness.

—Wallace D. Wattles

THE WISDOM TO SUCCEED

Wisdom alone is the science of other sciences.

—Plato

Wisdom is very important if you are to live a useful, fruitful, and fulfilled life. Though information and knowledge are relevant, wisdom encompasses all. It has been said in certain quarters that "information is power" or "knowledge is power." Such statements are not particularly true. The world today is awash with a fathomless degree of information and knowledge—the explosion and immeasurable activities of the Internet and social media and other inestimable technologies out there—yet we are not any wiser or safer.

Knowledge does not apply itself; we as individuals must make the application, and the application consists in fertilizing the thought with a living purpose.

—Charles Francis Haanel

SIXTH SENSE

To be truly successful, joyful, happy, wealthy, and prosperous with vibrant health, a healthy and loving family, and a healthy lifestyle overflowing with gratitude, love, and goodwill to all, we need more than information and knowledge.

> Wisdom does not show itself so much in precept as in life—in firmness of mind and a mastery of appetite. It teaches us to do as well as to talk and to make our words and actions all, of a color.
>
> —LUCIUS ANNAEUS SENECA

We need wisdom to comprehend that there is more to life than meets the eyes and to empower your sixth sense, the Super-divine-subconscious mind, to live above and beyond what you can see, hear, smell, taste, and touch.

> Wisdom is the power to perceive the best ends to aim at and the best means for reaching those ends.
>
> —WALLACE D. WATTLES

There are principles and steps one must follow and abide by if you are to make progress and succeed in life. There are principles and patterns to follow to understand how you can harness and apply the infinite Super-divine-subconscious mind latent in you for greater benefit and success in all areas. Once you understand the principles and acquire the habit, you can repeatedly and consistently harness and apply the infinite power of your Super-divine-subconscious mind for desired and deserved results in all areas of your life, positively!

> The way is long if one follows precepts, but short…if one follows patterns.
>
> —Lucius Annaeus Seneca

The universe and everything in it, including human beings, is energy. There are principles that govern every particle of energy in the universe. Just as there are no accidents or coincidences, there are only synchronicities. Synchronicity is described by *Merriam-Webster* as things (coincidences) that "happen to everyone sooner or later: A certain number pops up wherever you go; an old friend you haven't seen in twenty years since high school appears the same day you're looking at her picture in a yearbook; you're singing a song and turn on the radio—and the same song is playing."

There are formulas and processes to everything that never fail. Examples are all around us. For instance, in chemistry, it's proven that whenever you combine the atoms of hydrogen and oxygen, the result will always be water. Whenever you take one atom of oxygen and one atom of carbon and combine them, you will produce carbon monoxide, a poisonous gas. Whenever you add another atom of oxygen, you will get carbon dioxide, a gas that is harmless to animals and vital to plants. These are universal facts, irrefutable and unchangeable, and great examples of principles and natural law.

The principles of the infinite Super-divine-subconscious mind is no different from the workings of the principles of physics, mathematics, or chemistry. You must learn the principles applicable in any field to achieve success. Similarly, if you want to get the best out of your infinite Super-divine-subconscious mind, you must learn the principles. Just as water seeks its own level, so must you abide by the guiding principles of your infinite Super-divine-conscious mind to achieve greater success, balance, general well being, equanimity, and power.

Anyone can get results for a prayer when the attitude of the subconscious mind collides, passionately, with what is prayed for. In other words, whatever one passionately believes in with love and positive attitude becomes manifest. When you lovingly plant the seed of positivity in your infinite Super-divine-subconscious mind, through the principles of affirmation and with an open mind and strong belief, you will reap extraordinary harvest. You will be empowered beyond your comprehension. You will be able to harness and use the infinite potentials within you to add value to the world.

Through the principles of effective affirmation, you will be able to unlock and enhance your inner potentials to become more productive; add value to the world; create marvelous products, inventions, and discoveries; and make significant and positive difference in people's lives.

The conscious and subconscious mind operate by the law of belief. This means whatever your conscious mind thinks and receives from your subconscious mind becomes your prime belief. Belief is nothing but the thought in your mind.

> *Prayer is a thought, a belief, a feeling, arising within the mind of the one praying.*
>
> —Ernest Holmes

It is not the thing believed in but the belief in your mind that makes things happen. It is not the belief in a spiritual master, guru, prophet, Christ, Mohammed, pope, bishop, overseer, pastor, imam, herbalist, sticks, or stones, but the conscious thought that permeates your subconscious mind as belief that makes things happen.

> *In principle, the great religions of the world do not differ as much as they appear to.*
>
> —Ernest Holmes

Your current and past conditions, events, and experiences are caused by your subconscious reaction to your predominant thoughts. All your experiences, events, conditions, and acts are produced by your subconscious mind in reaction to your conscious thoughts.

I urge you to straight away cease from allowing any negative belief into your conscious mind. Don't give any room, time, or space in your infinite Super-divine-subconscious mind for superstitions, traditional limiting beliefs, prejudices, bigotry, pessimism, doubts, and fears that limit and hold many down and in bondage.

EUGENE N. NWOSU

I am tomorrow, or some future day, what I establish today. I am today what I established yesterday or some previous day.

—James Joyce

THE POTENT POWER OF THE "I AM, GOD IS, WE ARE ONE" PARADIGM

Each one of us is an outlet to God and an inlet to God.

—ERNEST HOLMES

START NOW TO believe in the miracle powers of the Infinite-divine-Universe, which you are part and parcel of. Awaken now and claim your unique and deserved right of place in the Infinite-divine-Universe. Know and strongly believe that you are one with the infinite universe because everything in the Infinite-divine-Universe is connected, including your mind, body, and spirit. The Infinite-divine-Universe is pure, unadulterated, positive love energy, God, and is connected to everything. Because we (humans), and everything in the universe is relatively connected with the Infinite-divine-Universal energy, being God's love; therefore, we are one with God!

I am, God is, we are one!

Once you comprehend and internalize this divine truth in your Super-divine-subconscious mind, I guarantee your paradigm will shift to greater heights. You will start to operate from illuminated, enlightened, and higher consciousness. You will be awakened and empowered to live your life with courage, strong self-control, and strength, with increased awareness, knowledge, wisdom, and mastery; above all, you will live your life with balance, calmness, and power—onward and God-ward. One thing is for sure: your life and entire existence shall never be the same again, going forward and upward, positively!

> You are a god in the company of gods and must conduct yourself accordingly.
>
> —WALLACE D. WATTLES

Anyone who reads this book with an open mind and earnestly and faithfully applies the affirmation principles and formulas is guaranteed to achieve positive results, balance, and success in all areas.

> To believe in a just law of cause and effect, carrying with it a punishment or a reward, is to believe in righteousness.
>
> —ERNEST HOLMES

Everything results from the universal law of action and reaction, or cause and effect. Every action is preceded by thought. Every reaction from the subconscious mind is in correspondence to the nature of your conscious thought. Therefore,

SIXTH SENSE

feed your subconscious mind with positive concepts of great and vibrant health, love, joy, peace, happiness, and goodwill to all, and great and wonderful things will begin to happen in your life and all around you.

You must consciously identify yourself with the infinite-divine-highest; being your infinite Super-divine-subconscious mind, Sixth Sense, by fully recognizing the fact that the infinite and divine power within you is the omnipotent, omnipresent, and omniscient God-energy.

> A noble and God-like character is not a thing of favor or chance but is the natural result of continued effort in right thinking, the effect of long-cherished association with God-like thoughts.
>
> —James Allen, *As a Man Thinketh*

TWO SIDES OF THE MIND

There are two sides to the mind, each with distinct characteristics and separate functions. They are essentially different from each other.

In recognition of the dynamic duality of the mind, several names and terminologies have been used to describe and differentiate the two mental functions. They include the inner and outer mind, the front and back of the mind, the waking and sleeping mind, the objective and subjective mind, the surface and deep self, the male and female mind, the voluntary and involuntary mind, and many other narratives.

In this book, as in most of my works, I refer to this dual universal energy as the conscious (outer) mind, encompassing the five physical senses of the human being, the subconscious (inner) mind, the sixth sense.

Briefly described, the conscious mind is very limited and operates within the confines of the five human senses—what we hear, see, taste, smell, and touch. The subconscious mind is the sixth sense; like a fertile garden or very powerful engine room, it has limitless and infinite powers. The conscious mind observes, collects, and delivers to the subconscious mind for response.

The subconscious mind, which I love to refer to as the infinite Super-divine-subconscious mind, is the sixth sense and is pure, soul, neutral, positive-love-energy, God's energy, and possesses limitless powers. It does not judge. It is very innocent and does not see anything as right or wrong, good or bad. It responds to everything in equal measure. It is neither young nor old; big nor small; blue, white, red, yellow, green, nor brown—it is everything to every gender, race, color, and creed and cannot be extinguished or die. It just translates and transforms into pure positive and divine-love-energy and remains the positive-love, universal God-energy, forever!

SIXTH SENSE

A man only begins to be himself when he ceases to whine and revile, and commences to search for the hidden justice which regulates his life. And he adapts his mind to that regulating factor, he ceases to accuse others as the cause of his condition, and builds himself up in strong and noble thoughts; ceases to kick against circumstances, but begins to use them as aids to his more rapid progress, and as a means of the hidden powers and possibilities within himself.

—JAMES ALLEN, *AS A MAN THINKETH*

THE CONSCIOUS AND SUBCONSCIOUS MIND AT WORK

LET'S BRIEFLY EXAMINE how the conscious and subconscious mind work. One of the great ways we can understand the dynamic roles of the two parts of the one mind is to use the simple and common analogy of the garden.

> A person's mind may be likened to a garden, which may be intelligently cultivated or allowed to run wild; but whether cultivated or neglected, it must, and will, bring forth. If no useful seeds are put into it, then an abundance of useless weed seeds will fall therein and will continue to produce their kind.
>
> —JAMES ALLEN, *As a Man Thinketh*

Let's assume that you and your conscious mind are the gardener, and your Super-divine-subconscious mind is the garden with very rich soil and fertile land. Through your conscious mind, you are planting seeds of thought in your subconscious mind all day long. There is so much happening every second in the day that you are collecting through your five senses; most of the time you are particularly unaware about your connection and contact with these incidences and how they go a long way to influence your habitual thoughts. The result or product of your conscious interactions and thoughts automatically gets down to your subconscious mind, the garden, as seeds.

The subconscious mind is a rich soil that will help any kind of seed, whether good or bad, to germinate, sprout, develop, grow, and blossom, thus validating the saying of "as you sow in your subconscious mind, so shall you reap in your body and environment!"

EUGENE N. NWOSU

As thy days, so shall thy strength be which, in modern language, may be translated as thy thoughts so shall thy life be.

—Emmet Fox

AS YOU SOW, SO SHALL YOU REAP!

> Though I do not believe that a plant will spring up where no seed has been, I have great faith in a seed. Convince me that you have a seed there, and I am prepared to expect wonders.
>
> —HENRY DAVID THOREAU

THE REALITY OF life is "you reap what you sow." It's the sacred law of the Infinite-divine-Universe. If you sow healthy seeds and healthy fruits, you shall harvest and reap healthy seeds and healthy fruits. If you sow grapes, you shall harvest and reap grapes; if you sow thorns, you shall expect thorns. If you sow pineapples and healthy beans, you shall harvest pineapples and healthy beans; if you sow thistles and unhealthy and harmful prickly plants, so shall you reap.

Simply put, thought is a cause, and condition is an effect. Every thought triggers something, and everything that happens is the effect of that initial thought. Therefore, it is very important that you take control of your thought process and consistently feed your subconscious with positive thoughts.

> It is the food which you furnish to your mind that determines the whole character of your life.
>
> —Emmet Fox

Start now to plant positive seeds in your Super-divine-subconscious mind. Begin now to sow the seeds of joy and happiness, peace, right action, love and goodwill to all, wealth, and prosperity in your Super-divine-subconscious mind. Consistently sow the seeds of greatness in the Infinite-Super-divine-subconscious of your mind, and you shall reap bountiful and glorious harvest.

When you understand the truth about the wonderful and infinite powers of your Super-divine-subconscious mind, your attitude and behavior will become constructive and virtuous.

You will begin to live your life in harmony with the natural laws of the Infinite-divine-Universe. You will live in harmonious conditions and agreeable surroundings and have access to the best of everything.

SIXTH SENSE

We begin to see, therefore, the importance of selecting our environment with the greatest of care, because environment is the mental feeding ground out of which the food that goes into our minds is extracted.

—Napoleon Hill

> Corrective learning begins with the awakening
> of spirit and the turning away from belief in
> physical sight.
>
> —Helen Schucman

Once you understand how to control your thought process, you can apply the powers of your subconscious to solve and ease your way through any problem or difficulty. You will be consciously cooperating with the infinite power of the divine universe and omnipotent and omnipresent laws that govern all things.

A lot of people in the world are not particularly aware of the powers of their subconscious mind, and they allow themselves to be manipulated, influenced, and controlled by outside circumstances and events. Many people live only by their five senses—what their conscious mind can hear, see, smell, taste, and touch.

> What lies behind us and what lies before us are
> tiny matters compared to what lies within us.
>
> —Ralph Waldo Emerson

The enlightened and truly successful human beings can live from the world within, achieving "inside out" balance. They have the awareness and ability to deliberately and consistently plant the seeds of positivity in their subconscious minds. They know that the world within, the Super-divine-subconscious mind, is the most powerful creative force.

SIXTH SENSE

Whatever image your conscious mind sees, feels, visualizes, and believes is what in turn becomes your experience. Everything that exists in your life was attracted by your conscious mind and planted in your subconscious, whether knowingly or unknowingly. Your mind is the maker of your world, and the choices you make uniquely establish your identity as you see and believe it.

> A person is buffeted by circumstances so long as he believes himself to be the creature of outside conditions, but when he realizes that he is a creative power, and that he may command the hidden soil and seeds of his being out of which circumstances grow, he then becomes the rightful master of himself.
>
> —JAMES ALLEN, *As a Man Thinketh*

When you comprehend the exciting reality about the connection and interface between your conscious and Super-divine-subconscious mind, your life will never be the same again, and you will have the choice and awesome ability to transform your entire life, positively, at will.

> Life is a mirror and will reflect, back to the thinker what he thinks into it.
>
> —ERNEST HOLMES

You must change the inner conditions of the mind if you wish to change your external conditions. Most people spend a lifetime of energy and resources trying to change circumstances and conditions by working on the circumstances and conditions that created the situations. They fail to see the connection. They fail to understand that all circumstances and conditions emanate from causes. They don't realize that their conditions flow from a cause.

To eliminate disharmony, strife, disorder, poverty, constraints, and limitations in your life, you must eliminate the cause. The way you allow your conscious mind to operate and the thought processes and images you allow into your conscious mind are the cause. Simply put, when you change the cause, the effect will change. If you want more joy and happiness, wealth and prosperity, peace and balance, calmness, tranquility, and power to overcome challenges and achieve unique success, the greater part of your life must be an inside job (inside out).

The world is full of an astonishing and limitless ocean of love and treasures. The subconscious is pure, innocent, neutral, sensitive, impressionable, and receptive of anything the conscious mind deposits to it.

SIXTH SENSE

> Why should we think upon things that are lovely? Because: thinking determines life. It is a common habit to blame life upon the environment. Environment modifies life but does not govern life. The soul is stronger than its surroundings.
>
> —WILLIAM JAMES

Your conscious thoughts form the medium through which the infinite intelligence, wisdom, dynamic forces, and energies of your subconscious flow. You can reprogram and redirect your conscious and subconscious mind to positively shape your environment for the better; achieve vibrant health; nurture a great and healthy family; have fulfilling and nourishing relationships, a healthy lifestyle, joy and happiness, balance, equilibrium, and calmness; and gain strength, mastery, and the power to triumph in all areas of your life.

> You have power over your mind—not outside events. Realize this, and you will find strength.
>
> —MARCUS AURELIUS

You will awaken and empower your conscious and Super-divine-subconscious mind to enable you to achieve wonderful successes. It is noteworthy to emphasis that most of the creative artists, inventors, outstanding musicians, writers, scientists, great business and political leaders, change agents of all generations, great teachers and lecturers, wonderful doctors and nurses, great and loving parents and caregivers, and great sports women and men were all able to awaken the infinite power of their conscious and Super-divine-subconscious minds in alignment with Infinite-divine-Universal principles, positively, for their awesome achievements and extraordinary successes.

> When you are inspired by some great purpose, some extraordinary project, all your thoughts break their bonds: your mind transcends limitations, your consciousness expands in every direction, and you find yourself in a new, great, and wonderful world. Dormant forces, faculties, and talents become alive, and you discover yourself to be a greater person than you ever dreamed yourself to be.
>
> —Patanjali

Your subconscious mind is responsive in nature and responds to the seed of thoughts planted by your conscious mind. Whenever your conscious mind is saddled with negative emotions, it triggers doubt, anxiety, distress, and apprehension in your subconscious mind. You can speak affirmatively and with a deep sense of authority and command to banish any negative and limiting emotions generated in your subconscious mind. You have the infinite power of control to command and direct your Super-divine-subconscious mind to act appropriately and per your needs.

SIXTH SENSE

Your subconscious responds to the command of your conscious mind and is referred to as a subjective mind because it is subject to the actions, seeds, and triggers of the conscious (objective) mind.

While reading this book, you will come across the most exceptional, influential, and empowering words distilled from lengthy and thorough scientific, spiritual, and empirical research, systematically and specifically formatted for you to positively reprogram and alter your subconscious mind. You will ignite and awaken the innate sense of awareness, illumination, enlightenment, wisdom, and paradigm shift for happiness, success, balance, equilibrium, and equanimity.

These self-proclamation and affirmations can be read aloud to oneself (by way of incantation) at least twice daily because the spoken word has awesome power, and the greatest power on earth is self-power. If this is done, the subconscious mind will be reprogrammed, the negative and limiting beliefs in the conscious mind will be replaced with these highly charged positive-oriented words, a paradigm shift in consciousness will take place, and one will gain automatic illumination, enlightenment, and above all, wisdom and intuitiveness for abundance and fulfillment in all areas.

These highly potent affirmation tools and autosuggestion formulas are arranged and organized scientifically and systematically to subliminally transform the Super-divine-subconscious mind for extreme and maximum effect and optimal result, designed and given out here in full and complete doses with no holds barred, for all who are ready and truly serious about changing their lives for positive results and greater good.

These are simple words you might be familiar with, and they may seem too simplistic at first glance. But I guarantee that if you start to repeat these words to yourself regularly, aloud in private or silently in public, for sixty days for maximum result or ninety days for optimal effectiveness, then you will gain miraculous powers and the freedom of choice to magically transform your life and achieve your heart's desires.

For maximum impact and optimal effectiveness, you might also use the optimal autosuggestion and affirmation tools and formulas in any or all the following ways:

- Use pen and paper and write the affirmation tools word by word, at least once or twice daily (in the morning and at night before bed). The simple act of writing these positive words engage and involve you holistically—physically, mentally, and spiritually—and give the entire exercise significant emotional impact, extra magic, and miraculous powers. You may alter them—rearrange the words or add stronger, more positive, and impactful words of your choice.
- You might record audio of these most powerful words in your own words. Words when spoken aloud have

great effect, and there is no greater sound in the universes that will override the sound of your own voice to your Super-divine-subconscious mind. Only the sound of your own voice can effectively and permanently replace old habits and plant a fresh and positive enhancing paradigm in your Super-divine-subconscious mind.

- All the audio hypnosis and subliminal recordings by other people that you might buy and use may work for you for a short while but would stop working when you stop listening to them. But when you take charge and record and listen to your own voice, you permanently create an undiluted, potent, and infinite subliminal-template of Super-divine-subconsciousness for the unique and divine you!

Create affirmations with these basic ingredients: they're personal, positive, in the present tense, visual, and emotional. Then, each day, visualize the realization of these affirmations. You'll find that your behavior and circumstances will change for the better.

—STEPHEN R. COVEY

THE WISDOM OF RESPONSIBILITY

"You are the architect of events in your life." All things are under your control. Realize now that you are in control; thus, you create and control everything in your life.

> We are made wise not by the recollection of our past, but by the responsibility for our future.
>
> —George Bernard Shaw

You are divine and part of the Infinite-divine-Universal energy, "the godhead." Your higher self, that Super-divine-subconsciousness in you, is the atom of God. God is in control of all things, and God is the higher self of all, which is your higher self—your soul. Therefore, all power is within you and absolutely under your control.

> The man who acquires the ability to take full possession of his own mind may take possession of anything else to which he is justly entitled.
>
> —Andrew Carnegie

Stop acting the victim; take responsibility and power for your life.

Your paradigm or mind-set creates events in your life. Through personal experience and life-long emphirical research and studies, I truly know and strongly believe everything that happens can be traced back to intention. Nothing happens outside of you. You are a Super-divine soul, atom of the Infinite-divine-Universal energy, the godhead and god-self. Your Super-divine-consciousness encompasses all that is.

> The outer conditions of a person's life will always be found to be harmoniously related to his inner state…Men do not attract that which they want, but that which they are.
>
> —James Allen, *As a Man Thinketh*

"I am responsible" is the most powerful autosuggestion that you can proclaim to take charge of the events in your life. The "I am responsible" creed will bring about a three-hundred-sixty-degree paradigm shift in your Super-divine-consciousness. Your entire world will be laid bare before your eyes. You will be illuminated, enlightened, and empowered to responsibly connect and align your inner self with your outer perceptions. You will subliminally apply discernment, empathy, compassion, tolerance, equity, truth, and justice in the choices you make and shall achieve the powerful wisdom of balance, equilibrium, and equanimity.

SIXTH SENSE

> Immense power is acquired by assuring yourself
> in your secret reveries that you were born to
> control affairs.
>
> —Andrew Carnegie

The entire universe and everything in it is energy based. You are part of that universal energy. You are part of everything, and all things relate to you. The most powerful thing in the universe is thought. Your intention, including feelings, desires, emotions, passion, wanting, willing, demanding, all have creative power. Each of these energy forces works within dual polarities: inward and outward, the desire-force (inward) and the will power (outward). These are referred to as motive pole and emotive pole, respectively, or feminine and masculine, and as in all dualities, a combination of both qualities and characteristics produces the awesome force. Together they become a very powerful creative power physically, mentally, and spiritually; thus, your desire translated into strong will is magical power.

> All day long the thoughts that occupy your mind,
> your secret place as Jesus calls it, are molding
> your destiny for good or evil; in fact, the truth is
> that the whole of our life's experience is but the
> outer expression of inner thought.
>
> —Emmet Fox

EMPOWERING QUESTION TO THE SUBCONSCIOUS

It is not in the stars to hold our destiny but in ourselves.

—WILLIAM SHAKESPEARE

IF YOU REPEAT these empowering questions daily, you will awaken and enliven the infinite intelligence of your Super-divine-subconscious mind, and you will have the subliminal clarity of purpose to engage in creative and worthy ideals:

- What am I willing to do today to make things the way I want them?
- What am I willing to no longer do today to make things the way I want them?
- How can I enjoy the process today while I do what is necessary to make things the way I want them?
- Because I am in conscious unity with that within me that is the Infinite-divine highest, I will obey my soul and be true to that within me that is the infinite highest. I am the supreme master of my Super-divine-subconscious mind, and I am, God is, and we are one!

SIXTH SENSE

> Follow effective action with quiet reflection. From the quiet reflection, will come even more effective action.
>
> —Peter Drucker

WHAT WE FOCUS UPON EXPANDS

> Your ability to use the principle of autosuggestion will depend, very largely, upon your capacity to concentrate upon a given desire until that desire becomes a burning obsession.
>
> —NAPOLEON HILL

I URGE YOU to make a serious commitment now for your overall self-improvement and development—memorize and regularly repeat the very powerful words (as proclamation, affirmation, autosuggestion, or scientific prayer) in the previous chapter to permanently reprogram and instill the essential and significant paradigm shift and positively uplift, unlock, and unleash the optimal power within your Super-divine-subconscious. This will add greater value to yourself, your nearest and dearest, and the world, and overall, will help you achieve greater health, abundant wealth, peace, happiness, balance, equilibrium, and equanimity for the rest of your life.

SIXTH SENSE

Direct your eye inward and you'll find
a thousand regions in your mind yet
undiscovered. Travel them, and be expert in
home-cosmography.

—Henry David Thoreau

WORDS HAVE TREMENDOUS POWER

> The "I" of you is not the physical body. That is simply an instrument which the "I" uses to carry out its purposes.
>
> —CHARLES FRANCIS HAANEL

THE MOST POWERFUL and influential one-letter word anyone can use as an opening sentence for magical and positive effect is *I*. The subconscious responds to the command of the conscious mind. Whatever word that comes out of your mouth goes a long way to form your reality and affects the world around you, whether you know it or not.

> I believe that there is a subtle magnetism in nature, which, if we unconsciously yield to it, will direct us aright.
>
> —HENRY DAVID THOREAU

The infinite universe and everything in it is energy, and all are connected to the omnipotent and omnipresent love-energy, God. You and I are part and parcel of the entire infinite

SIXTH SENSE

love-energy, God. You are, I am, and we are one with the Infinite-divine-Universal love-energy, God!

> Life isn't about finding yourself. Life is about creating yourself.
>
> —GEORGE BERNARD SHAW

Whenever you say the word *I*, you automatically assert your unique authority as a significant being and part of the universal love-energy, God's. Whatever word or sentence you say or express after *I* form your reality in the world. The past and present conditions you live in have all been due to how you might have used the most spiritual and powerful *I*. Here is an example of some of the things that you might have added to the all-powerful, infinite, divine, and spiritual *I*: I am, I will, I wish, I desire, I deserve, I can, I can't, I could, I couldn't.

> So long as a man is faithful to himself, everything is in his favor, government, society, the very sun, moon, and stars.
>
> —HENRY DAVID THOREAU

You are responsible for most of your past and present successes and limitations because of the conditions of your thought. Whatever you thought, said to yourself, and believed are what formed your perceptions, which turned out to become your reality. You have all along been responsible for the world you live in.

Your awakening and empowering moment begins the moment you accept responsibility for your past and present situation. Become accountable; start now to acknowledge and appreciate your unique and important place in the Infinite-divine-Universe.

You have the awareness and enlightenment now to go forward and proclaim that you are love-energy and an integral part of the omnipotent and omnipresent, God.

> Your real self—the "I am I"—is master of this land, the ruler of this empire. You rightfully have power and dominion over it, all its inhabitants, and all contained in its realm.
>
> —Robert Collier

You know now that you are responsible for your present, past, and future. Start now to be accountable for your current and future situations.

You know now that you are powerful, that you are a winner, that you have always been winning.

Declare now that you are financially independent and financially free, and so it shall be.

Affirm now that you are healthy, wealthy, rich, and prosperous, and so it shall be.

SIXTH SENSE

Decree now that you have a great and healthy family, and so it shall be.

Proclaim now that joy, happiness, love, peace, love and goodwill to all, power, wisdom, and extraordinary successes all flow in and through you, through infinite and multiple stream of choices, in avalanches of abundance, freely, copiously, and endlessly. You are in conscious unity with that within you that is the Infinite-divine highest; you will obey your soul and be true to that within you that is the Infinite-divine highest; you are the supreme master of your Super-divine-subconscious mind because you are, God is, and we are one.

You are now in a very powerful position to direct your life appropriately, add value to and help shape the world around you, and make significant and positive differences in life.

Start now to make the most of your awareness and enlightenment by following through with strong belief and firm commitments.

EUGENE N. NWOSU

Do not merely think that you are great; think that you are great now. Do not think that you will begin to act in a great way at some future time; begin now.

—Wallace D. Wattles

AFFIRMATION CHALLENGE

HERE'S AN AFFIRMATION challenge for your incantation and scientific prayer to facilitate, awaken, and empower the infinite powers of your Super-divine-subconscious mind. Harness and apply these positive words to help you achieve overall self-control and strength, self-awareness, knowledge, wisdom, and mastery, and above all balance, equilibrium, calmness, and power.

> Every great dream begins with a dreamer.
> Always remember, you have within you the
> strength, the patience, and the passion to reach
> for the stars to change the world.
>
> —HARRIET TUBMAN

Whatever you say to yourself is what becomes your reality. Go ahead and challenge yourself and strongly commit these simple positive affirmations to your Super-divine-subconscious mind. Train your conscious mind to memorize these words by way of repetitive incantation and in the strongest terms possible. You can boldly add any superlative words of your choice for a stronger, positive effect. You may rearrange, calibrate, and reformat them for your convenience and comfort.

> I am love. I am responsible. I am accountable. I am powerful. I am a winner. I am winning. I am financially independent. I am financially free. I am financially successful. I truly and deeply know and strongly believe that in my own Infinite-divine-Universe, I am truly and deeply worthy of all my desires. I am ever so very grateful. I am ever so very happy. I am ever so much fulfilled. I am so very excited now that I truly and deeply know and strongly believe that in my own Infinite-divine-Universe, wealth, riches, prosperity, health, happiness, joy, love, freedom, peace, a great and healthy family, love and goodwill for all, power, wisdom, and extraordinary success all flow in and through me, through an infinite and multiple stream of choices, in avalanches of abundance, freely, copiously, and endlessly because I am in conscious unity with that within me that is the infinite divine highest. I will obey my soul, and I will be true to that within me that is the Infinite-divine highest because I am the supreme master of my Super-divine-subconscious mind. I am, God is, we are one!

> *If you desire a thing, picture it clearly and hold the picture steadily in mind until it becomes a definite thought-form.*
>
> —Wallace D. Wattles

YOU CAN DO ALL THINGS!

Whatsoever things that are true, whatsoever things that are honest, whatsoever things that are just, whatsoever things that are pure, whatsoever things that are lovely, whatsoever things that are of good report; if there be any virtue, and if there be any praise, think and live on these things.

—Phil. 4:8 (Biblical, KJ21)

You can do all things through the infinite intelligence of your Super-divine-subconscious mind. The infinite intelligence of your Super-divine-subconscious soul is the human spirit and part of the universal love-energy, God, and all connected.

The infinite intelligence of your Super-divine-subconscious mind thrives on excellence, superior engagements, quality pursuits, and brilliant expectations. Your goals and desires must be true, honest, pure, loving, virtuous, big, and exciting enough if you are to unlock the infinite creative power of your Super-divine-subconscious mind for greater achievements and successes in all areas of your life.

> There is in this world no such force as the force
> of a person determined to rise. The human
> soul cannot be permanently chained.
>
> —W.E.B. Dubois

You have now the illumination, enlightenment, awareness, and tools to empower the infinite love-energy of your Super-divine-subconscious mind for the answer to all your desires. The treasure house within you is the ocean of love and mercy, positive universal love-energy, and God's love.

> You are already one with God; you want to
> become consciously aware of it.
>
> —Wallace D. Wattles

You possess now the same ability to connect, harness, and draw from the infinite powers of the Super-divine-subconscious mind that was the greatest secret possessed by great men and women of all ages.

The infinite intelligence of your Super-divine-subconscious mind has the answer to all your situations. Whatever you suggest to your subconscious, it carries out without hesitation or question.

EMPOWERED AND HEALTHY SUBCONSCIOUS MIND

The wish for healing has always been half of health.

—Lucius Annaeus Seneca

THE INFINITE INTELLIGENCE of your Super-divine-subconscious mind, soul, is a particle of the universal love-energy, God; it is the builder of your body and can heal you. Implant the ideas of excellent and vibrant health to your subconscious mind regularly, particularly before you go to sleep every night, and your subconscious will faithfully respond and deliver.

The infinite intelligence of your Super-divine-subconscious mind is a very powerful force within your control. Your subconscious mind is the most powerful, creative, building, and healing force in your possession. This precious and most powerful force is soul, the real you; it is the infinite divine spirit, omnipotent and omnipresent, positive-love-energy, God, of which you and I are a particle.

Your subconscious is the real you, soul; it is infinite, Super-divine-subconscious, Holy Spirit, universal positive-love-energy, God. The human body and conscious mind are a significant cloak and important vehicles for the soul in the physical universe. Therefore, the real you, soul, is a spirit in a human body with your conscious mind as the captain and navigator. It is always with you, and its most wonderful power is ready and always available to serve you. All you need to do is master how to consistently sow positive seeds into it, and you shall reap bountiful rewards.

> The more man meditates upon good
> thoughts, the better will be his world and
> the world at large.
>
> —Confucius

We know now that there are two levels to the mind—the conscious, objective, and lucid level, and the subconscious, subjective, and illogical level. We think and reason with the conscious mind, and whatever we consistently think is planted in our subconscious mind, which then subliminally responds, sprouts, and develops per the nature of our thoughts.

The subconscious mind is the seat of our emotions. It is the fertile, creative, and abundant garden for the mind, and by the infinite divine law of the universe, if we think and plant good, we reap good. If we think and plant evil, evil becomes manifest in our lives.

SIXTH SENSE

It is vital to point out that once the subconscious mind accepts an idea, it starts to execute it without hesitation. The subconscious is neutral in nature; it reacts and responds to good and bad ideas equally and works for good and bad ideas impartially. Therefore, when applied in a negative way, it causes sadness, doubt, failure, stress, anger, hatred, frustration, and deficiency. However, when the attitude of mind is peaceful, positive, loving, and joyful, we experience excellent and vibrant health, peace, joy and happiness, and wealth and prosperity.

> All the breaks you need in life wait within your imagination; imagination is the workshop of your mind, capable of turning mind energy into accomplishment and wealth.
>
> —Napoleon Hill

Whatever you affirm mentally and truly believe, your subconscious mind will accept and make it your experience and reality. Healthy body, peace, joy, and happiness are certain once you begin to reason and impress your conscious mind with optimistic and positive feelings. Once your Super-divine-subconscious mind receives the constructive and positive idea, it will appropriately respond in return with all that you need for excellent and vibrant health, peace, joy and happiness, and prosperity.

Neuroscientists, psychologists and psychiatrists have proven that when thoughts are conveyed to the subconscious mind, impressions are made in the brain cells. In other words, any idea or thought that the conscious mind conceives automatically goes to the subconscious; the subconscious always admits the idea and immediately puts it into effect. And in collaboration, the subconscious gathers every bit of information from your lifetime experience and knowledge to fulfill its mandate. It draws from the Infinite-divine-Universal power, positive love-energy, ocean of love and mercy, God, within you to make your desires come true.

You may sometimes receive immediate solutions to your difficulties, but at other times, it may take longer—weeks, days, months, or more. One thing you can be sure of is that the Infinite-divine-Universe in collaboration with your Super-divine-subconscious mind will reward you accordingly and appropriately. You shall reap the fruits of the seeds you sowed. The infinite power of your Super-divine-subconscious mind in collaboration with the positive love-energy of the universe will reward you with your just deserved. It is the divine law of the universe that everyone gets what he or she deserves at the appropriate time.

SIXTH SENSE

You may think that you are well, but you will not secure health until you think thoughts that produce health. You may persistently affirm that you are well, but so long as you live in discord, confusion, worry, fear, and other wrong states of mind, you will be sick; that is, you will be as you think and not what you think you are. You may state health in your thought, but if you give worry, fear, and discord to that thought, your thinking will produce discord. It is not what we state in our thoughts, but what we give to our thoughts that determine results.

—Christian D. Larson

AFFIRMATION FOR HEALING AND VIBRANT HEALTH

> When the mind becomes so completely absorbed in perfect health that all sickness is forgotten, all the powers of mind will proceed to create health, and every trace of sickness will soon disappear. When the mind becomes so completely absorbed in higher attainments and in greater achievements that all thought of failure is forgotten, all the forces of mind will begin to work for the promotion of those attainments and achievements. The person will be gaining ground every day, and greater success will positively follow.
>
> —Christian D. Larson

YOUR BODY AND all its organs were created by the infinite intelligence of your Super-divine-subconscious mind. It knows how to heal you. Its wisdom fashioned all your organs, tissues, muscles, and bones. This infinite healing presence within you will transform every cell of your being, making you whole and perfect. Memorize and adopt the following affirmation for vibrant health and general well being.

> I am ever so very grateful; I am ever so very happy; I am ever so much fulfilled; and I am ever so very excited now that I truly and deeply know and strongly believe that in my own Infinite-divine-Universe, my body and all its organs were created by the infinite intelligence of my Super-divine-subconscious mind. It knows how to heal me. Its wisdom fashioned all my organs, tissues, muscles, and bones. This infinite healing presence within me is now transforming every cell of my being, making me whole and perfect. I give thanks for the healing I know is taking place now. Wonderful are the works of the creative intelligence within me because I am in conscious unity with that within me that is the Infinite-divine highest. I will obey my soul and be true to that within me that is the Infinite-divine highest because I am the supreme master of my Super-divine-subconscious mind. I am, God is, we are one!

EMPOWERED AND CREATIVE CONSCIOUSNESS

Our ambition should be to rule ourselves, the true kingdom for each one of us; and true progress is to know more, and be more, and to do more.

—OSCAR WILDE

EVERY THOUGHT IS a cause, and every condition is an effect. The Infinite-divine-Universe is governed by definite, impartial, constant, holistic, and irrefutable laws. Thus, we live in a very orderly, precise, and dynamic universe, and we succeed or fail in proportion to our adherence to laws of the Infinite-divine-Universe.

When you become passionately engaged in the life and work of your dreams, in alignment with the Infinite-divine-Universal laws, you will succeed all the time.

SIXTH SENSE

You have that within you which is ever impelling you toward the upward and advancing way; and that impelling something is the divine Principle of Power; you must obey it without question.

—WALLACE D. WATTLES

One thing that is certain is the laws of the Infinite-divine-Universe are constantly working, whether you know it and whether they seem fair. It may not be fair that a young child falls when he or she is learning to walk, but the law of gravity is at work day and night, whether the young child is sleeping or trying to take first steps, and whether he or she even understands gravity. The laws operate whether you know about them or use them consciously, so you might as well take hold of them and put them to work for you to deliberately and positively steer and direct your career, relationships, health, spirituality, and finances toward greater good.

Success is a never-ending journey; it is not a specific destination. It is a process that mostly depends on the direction of your choice. It is your progressive journey toward your highest purpose, based on your vision, dreams, and desires in all areas of your life. Just as the great author and philosopher Earl Nightingale once said, "Success is the progressive realization of a worthy ideal." That means that success is a never-ending experience, an ever-unfolding awareness and enlightenment, and ever-growing wisdom.

> We become just by performing just action,
> temperate by performing temperate actions,
> brave by performing brave action.
>
> —Aristotle

Begin now to craft and create a bigger vision for yourself. Start now to look at life with an open mind; have a broader perspective of life and see the bigger picture.

Let your conscious mind dwell more on creative, productive, inspirational, motivational, and positive things.

Everything in the Infinite-divine-Universe is energy and all connected. Thought is one of the most powerful and influential forms of energy, and it vibrates at the highest of frequencies. Your thoughts and feelings are things.

Every thought and feeling creates a vibration, an impulse of energy that goes out into the Infinite-divine-Universe and stays there forever. That is why we attract to us the things we focus on, think about, and give energy to.

> The happiness of your life depends upon the quality of your thoughts: therefore, guard accordingly, and take care that you entertain no notions unsuitable to virtue and reasonable nature.
>
> —Marcus Aurelius

SIXTH SENSE

What you think about, you bring about. When you think positive thoughts, you attract positive people and circumstances to you. When you think negative thoughts, you attract negative people and circumstances.

Here's a powerful affirmation formula to further enliven and enrich your creativity:

I am love; I am responsible; I am accountable; I am powerful; I am a winner; I am winning; I am financially independent; I am financially free; I am financially successful; and I truly and deeply know and strongly believe that in my own Infinite-divine-Universe, I am one with the infinite intelligence of my Super-divine-subconscious mind, which knows no obstacles, difficulty, or delay.

I live in the joyous expectancy of the best. My deeper mind responds to my thoughts. I know that the work of the infinite power of my Super-divine-subconscious mind cannot be hindered. Infinite intelligence always finishes successfully whatever it begins.

Creative wisdom works through me, bringing all my plans and purposes to completion. Whatever I start, I bring to a successful conclusion.

My aim in life is to give wonderful service, and all those whom I contact are blessed by what I have, to offer. All my work comes to full fruition in divine order because I am in conscious unity with that within me that is the Infinite-divine highest. I will obey my soul and be true to that within me that is the Infinite-divine highest because I am the supreme master of my Super-divine-subconscious mind. I am, God is, we are one!

SIXTH SENSE

Think only of what you desire, and expect only what you desire, even when the very contrary seems to be coming into your life. Make it a point to have definite results in mind, always. Permit no thinking to be aimless. Every aimless thought is time and energy wasted, while every thought that is inspired with a definite aim will help to realize that aim, and if all your thoughts are inspired with a definite aim, the whole power of your mind will be for you and will work with you in realizing what you have in view. That you should succeed is therefore assured, because there is enough power in your mind to realize your ambitions, provided all, of that power is used in working for your ambitions.

—Christian D. Larson

LIKE ATTRACTS LIKE

Any idea that is held in the mind that is emphasized, feared, or revered will begin at once to clothe itself in the most convenient and appropriate physical form that is available.

—Napoleon Hill

WHATEVER YOU FEED your subconscious mind grows. Every thought you think attracts to you things that are like them. Your conscious thoughts can attract your dreams or your fears. If you think about your dreams, you will attract them. If you think about your fears, you will attract the things you fear.

When one has the feeling of dislike for evil, when one feels tranquil, one finds pleasure in listening to good teachings; when one has these feelings, and appreciates them, one is free of fear.

—Buddha

SIXTH SENSE

You naturally move toward what you focus your conscious thought on and move away from anything that is unlike the thoughts you are thinking. If you spend most of your time focusing on what you don't want, you will move toward that. If you think about what you do want, you will move toward that. By the same token, you can repel negativity by thinking positively.

EUGENE N. NWOSU

The key to growth is the introduction of higher dimensions of consciousness into our awareness.

—Lao Tzu

LOOK FOR THE GOOD!

Happiness is when what you think, what you say, and what you do are in harmony.

—MAHATMA GANDHI

EVERYTHING IN OUR material world is made real only by a relationship to something else. Hot exists only because we compare it to cold. Good exists only in comparison to bad.

Everything in life "just is"—unless and until we compare things to something else. Nothing in life has any intrinsic meaning except the meaning we give it.

Our perception of incidences and events and how we compare ourselves may be uplifting or self-defeating. How you view and interpret events and how you choose to compare yourself and your success either pulls you up or holds you down. Start now to see every incidence and event in your life as just another situation and opportunity to learn and grow. Begin now to acknowledge, appreciate, and be grateful for everything in your life. There is good in every situation; if you look hard enough, you will find it, positively!

> The marvelous richness of human experience
> would lose something of rewarding joy if there
> were no limitations to overcome. The hilltop
> hour would not be half so wonderful if there
> were no dark valleys to traverse.
>
> —Helen Keller

Everything in the Infinite-divine-Universe has an opposite, and nothing can exist without its opposite. Bad must exist for us to appreciate good. Where hate exists, then love must exist as well. When we see low potential in someone, then high potential must also exist in that person. Failure in life must be accompanied by the seeds of Success. If something is awful, then the possibility must exist for it to be awesome. These opposites are simply different manifestations of the same thing!

> Every adversity, every failure, every heartache
> carries with it the seed of an equal or greater
> benefit.
>
> —Napoleon Hill

My own personal trials, tribulations, and failures have been some of the most powerful experiences of my life and have given me the tools and wisdom I needed to succeed.

Without failure, it is difficult to know success. When you hear, most successful people talk about how they got where they are, you do not hear them say that they just woke up one morning and looked up at the sky and success poured onto them. Rather, their stories are full of how they were humbled by their failures and how their failures made them wiser and more determined to succeed.

> Experience is one thing you can't get for nothing.
>
> —OSCAR WILDE

You may know about the story of the young man who asked the wise old man: "How did you get to be so wise?"

The wise old man answered: "Well, by making wise choices."

"How did you know they were wise choices?" the young man countered.

"By experience, of course," the old man replied.

"How did you get experience?" the young man asked.

"By making mistakes!" the wise old man said.

Knowing that every challenging experience contains the seeds of its opposite—success—confirms that life is a constant learning experience and a fascinating and wonderful journey.

EUGENE N. NWOSU

> Life is a series of experiences, each one of which makes us bigger, even though sometimes it is hard to realize this. For the world was built to develop character, and we must learn that the setbacks and griefs which we endure help us in our marching onward.
>
> —HENRY FORD

NOTHING STAYS THE SAME

> Observe constantly that all things take place by change, and accustom thyself to consider that the nature of the universe loves nothing so much as to change the things which are, and to make new things like them.
>
> —Marcus Aurelius

THE INFINITE ENERGY of the divine-universe rhythmically swings like a pendulum. The Infinite-divine-Universe is methodically designed so that whenever something swings to the right, it must also swing to the left. Everything in existence in this amazing universe is involved in this rhythmical dance—swaying, flowing, swinging back and forth. Nothing stays the same; everything is either growing or diminishing, moving forward or backward, progressing or regressing, living or dying!

> Nature gives to every time and season some beauties of its own; and from morning to night, as from the cradle to the grave, it is but a succession of changes so gentle and easy that we can scarcely mark their progress.
>
> —Charles Dickens

Everything about the Infinite-divine-Universe is synchronized and orderly. The seasons come and go. The sun rises and sets. The sea ebbs and flows with synchronized high and low tides. Even our moods and levels of awareness swing back and forth. We have high and lows—intellectually, emotionally, and physically. Everything from relationships to the business enterprise goes through cycles in a rhythmic pattern. Great leaders have used their understanding of this law to predict their own declines or their greatest victories. When something is at its peak, they realize that it will soon start to swing back the other way. You probably use this law without even being aware of doing so. If you've been putting out a lot of effort in exercise, training, and workouts, you always get to moments when your body may need a rest. This pattern shows up in everyone's lives all the time, just as in the act of going to sleep and waking up. You use it when you get a gut feeling or an intuitive response, whether this is a good time to act on something or whether you should wait.

SIXTH SENSE

*Success is a science; if you have the conditions,
you get the result.*

—Oscar Wilde

The Infinite-divine-Universe is in a perpetual and never-ending cycle. It is the divine order of the infinite universe that every effect must have a cause, and every cause must have an effect. Anything that is a cause is the effect of something that came before it. And that effect becomes the cause of something else. It is impossible to start a new chain of events.

All religious and spiritual philosophies speak of the law of cause and effect, or the law of karma. They may phrase it in a variety of ways, such as the following:

- What you sow, so shall you reap.
- If you put a lot in, you get a lot back.
- You can't get back something other than what you give.
- You can't grow potatoes by planting corn—and you can't reap diamonds by planting rocks.
- What goes around, comes around.
- As you give, so shall you receive.

What we think about, we bring about. This is the ultimate in cause and effect, and it can happen not just in our individual lives but in groups and organizations and countries and nations.

Remember, nothing happens by chance in this Infinite-divine-Universe. When you succeed, there is a specific cause for your success.

> Adapt yourself to the things among which your lot has been cast and love sincerely the fellow creatures with whom destiny has ordained that you shall live.
>
> —MARCUS AURELIUS

An important factor in the creative process is the concept of yin and yang, or male and female order, which must unite for creation to take place. Also, there must be preparation period, planting of the seed period, or incubation and gestation period.

The implication is that everything new is merely the result of things that already existed but in a changed form. In this sense, nothing is ever created or destroyed. Everything is energy and the same; therefore, nothing ever dies. Infinite-divine energy just changes form to re-create itself.

> Life is a series of natural and spontaneous changes. Don't resist them—that only creates sorrow. Let reality be reality. Let things flow naturally forward in whatever way they like.
>
> —LAO TZU

SIXTH SENSE

All the success you want in life already exists in this Infinite-divine-Universe. There is only one source of supply—the Infinite-divine-Universal love-energy, God, which is omnipotent and omnipresent and a positive ocean of love and mercy!

> If you realize that all things change, there is nothing you will try to hold on to. If you are not afraid of dying, there is nothing you cannot achieve.
>
> —Lao Tzu

The fact that everything comes from and is made up of the same Infinite-divine-Universal love-energy, God, means that everything that you desire already exists. It may currently be in a different form, but it is nevertheless here in the Infinite-divine-Universe. There is nothing to create. All you need to do is to access and harness it, manifest and bring it forth, for greater good.

We are spiritual beings in human bodies, and the physical world we experience is only a small part of our true existence. To become successful and stay successful, we must stay connected with the source of all success.

We must have faith in the unseen reality. True faith is the ability to believe and trust in the unseen. Rather than waiting until you see it to believe it, begin to believe it until you see it!

We do this more easily and often than we realize. At this moment, the room you are in is full of radio waves and wireless Internet frequencies (Wi-Fi). You know those radio waves and Wi-Fi are there, even though you can't see them. You know that if you turned on a radio, television, phone, or computer, you will receive a signal, hear the radio, watch television, or use the Internet on your phone or computer. All you must do is switch on, tune in, and log on to the right frequency.

But remember, everything has its preparation, incubation, and gestation period—and we don't always know how long that period is in the unseen, nonphysical, spiritual realm. For instance, in the physical world, we know that it takes nine months to have a baby. It would be silly for the father to go up to the mother in her fourth month and say, "Where's the baby?! Is this going to work or not?" Yet that's just what we often do when we're working on the nonphysical plane because our information isn't quite as exact in that realm as it is in the physical world.

> Before success comes in any man's life, he is sure to meet with much temporary defeat and perhaps some failures. When defeat overtakes a man, the easiest and the most logical thing to do is to quit. That's exactly what the majority, of men do.
>
> —NAPOLEON HILL

SIXTH SENSE

People who fail to win in life usually give up just when something is just about to break through for them. They plant the seed and wait for it to manifest, but when it's just about to break through the ground, they lose patience, give up, and miss out on the opportunity for success that was just few moments away.

> Effort only fully releases its reward after a person refuses to quit.
>
> —Napoleon Hill

Faith and belief are dynamic ingredients for success. Belief and faith are always at the core of every success story. If you plant the seed of positivity, with genuine and true faith and a strong belief in the infinite powers of your Super-divine-subconscious mind, you shall reap extraordinary and bountiful results.

Plant the seed, have faith and strong belief, and wait. Your success will come, just as surely as the baby does after nine months. You must turn on your radio and tune in to the right frequency. What you are seeking is also seeking you.

EUGENE N. NWOSU

Be content with what you have; rejoice in the way things are. When you realize, there is nothing lacking, the whole world belongs to you.

—Lao Tzu

CHANGE YOUR SUBCONSCIOUS THOUGHTS–CHANGE YOUR RESULTS!

The man who acquires the ability to take full possession of his own mind may take possession of anything else to which he is justly entitled.

—ANDREW CARNEGIE

CHANGE YOUR SUBCONSCIOUS thoughts, and you change your destiny. Every successful person knows that when it comes to success, the past does not dictate the future. The past does not, really, equal the future. Many people get discouraged and demoralized when they look at what has happened so far in their lives.

If you are using your current results to measure who you are and how successful you can be, you may be limiting yourself and even damaging your chances for future success. It would be like driving and figuring out where to turn by considering the rear-view mirror instead of focusing on the road ahead of you.

> A chain is no stronger than its weakest link, and
> life is after all a chain.
>
> —William James

Your current situation is the direct result of your past subconscious thoughts, choices, and actions. You will get the same results again and end up with more of whatever you have now if you look at your current situation and make decisions about who you are and what you can have based on those results. You would be applying and repeating the same subconscious thoughts, choices, and actions that got you where you are today.

> Don't go around saying the world owes you a living. The world owes you nothing. It was here first.
>
> —Mark Twain

The number one principle and most revolutionary and empowering concept that you can adopt to transform your entire future is this: Change your subconscious thoughts, positively, and change your life, positively, for greater good.

SIXTH SENSE

> There is, as Emerson says, some central idea
> or conception of yourself by which all the
> facts of your life are arranged and classified.
> Change this central idea and you change the
> arrangement or classification of all the fact and
> circumstances of your life.
>
> —WALLACE D. WATTLES

When you change your subconscious thoughts, you will change your results. If you acknowledge and appreciate this simple principle, with an open mind, good faith, and strong belief in the infinite powers of your Super-divine-subconscious mind, you will change your life beyond your comprehension and for greater good, and you will achieve balance, joy and happiness, self-control and strength, enlightenment and self-awareness, knowledge, wisdom, and mastery, and above all, equanimity, calmness, and power.

> Pessimism leads to weakness, optimism to
> power.
>
> —WILLIAM JAMES

Your true success begins only when you turn away from the things you don't want and begin to focus on what you do want. So, surround yourself with higher and positive energy most of the time.

Whatever you want to accomplish, communicate that desire passionately and lovingly to your Super-divine-subconscious mind, and it will respond accordingly and appropriately.

> If you do not change direction, you may end up where you are heading.
>
> —Lao Tzu

Your conscious mind is like a captain navigating a ship. It must give the right orders, or the ship is wrecked. In the same way, your conscious mind must give the right orders (thoughts and images) to your subconscious mind, which controls and governs all your experiences.

Refrain from using words such as "can't afford it," "can't do this," or "can't do that." Your subconscious mind takes you at your word and delivers in equal measure without questions or hesitation. It sees to it that you get what you commanded.

> We are what we think. All that we are arises with our thoughts. With our thoughts, we make the world.
>
> —Buddha

For your own greater good, go on now and awaken and empower your Super-divine-subconscious mind with the following

SIXTH SENSE

affirmation: "I truly and deeply know and strongly believe that in my own Infinite-divine-Universe, I can do all things through the infinite power of my Super-divine-subconscious mind."

Believe your greatness!

The core of your life is wrapped around the principle of belief. Belief is a thought in your conscious mind. Whatever you believe becomes your reality. Start now to believe more in positive things that can bring you more joy and happiness, love, peace, and tranquility. Begin to believe more in the infinite power of your Super-divine-subconscious mind to heal you, to inspire and strengthen you, and to give you peace and prosperity, and it shall be done unto you, per your belief!

He who conquers others is strong; he who conquers himself is mighty.

—LAO TZU

Below are further positive affirmations to awaken and empower the infinite power of your Super-divine-subconscious mind for greater good. Memorize and plant these powerful words in the infinite garden of your Super-divine-subconscious mind. Meditate upon them, use them as a form of incantation or prayer, write them out and read them aloud to yourself several times a day, or tape record and listen to them.

If you faithfully practice these affirmations with an open mind and truly believe and trust the infinite power of your Super-divine-subconscious mind, you will be empowered to achieve all your heart's desires.

I truly and deeply know and strongly believe that in my own Infinite-divine-Universe, the infinite intelligence of my Super-divine subconscious that gave me these desires leads, guides, and reveals to me the perfect plan and solution for the unfolding, accomplishment, achievement, and fulfillment of my desires.

I truly and deeply know and strongly believe that in my own Infinite-divine-Universe, the wisdom of my Super-divine subconscious is responding to me now, and what I feel and claim within is expressed and made manifest in the without. There is a balance, equilibrium, and equanimity because I am in conscious unity with that within me that is the Infinite-divine highest. I will obey my soul and be true to that within me that is the Infinite-divine highest because I am the supreme master of my Super-divine-subconscious mind. I am, God is, we are one!

SIXTH SENSE

Why should we think upon things that are lovely? Because: thinking determines life. It is a common habit to blame life upon the environment. Environment modifies life but does not govern life. The soul is stronger than its surroundings.

—William James

THE TWO SCOPES OF THE ONE MIND

The formation of one's character ought to be everyone's chief aim.

—Johann Wolfgang von Goethe

THE CONSCIOUS AND subconscious are not two minds. They are merely two scopes of activity within the one mind. The conscious mind is the reasoning mind. It is that segment of the mind that chooses. For instance, you apply your conscious mind to choose your relationship, your home, your clothes, your food, the books you read, and so on. You make all your choices with your conscious mind.

Your subconscious mind is the core of your being. It is pure energy, infinite, omnipotent, and omnipresent, and, astonishingly, without any conscious choice on your part through independent processes, your subconscious has infinite capacity to keep your heart and vital organs functioning and keep you breathing, even in your sleep when your conscious mind is inactive.

SIXTH SENSE

The world we see that seems so insane is the result of a belief system that is not working. To perceive the world differently, we must be willing to change our belief system, let the past slip away, expand our sense of now, and dissolve the fear in our minds.

—WILLIAM JAMES

The subconscious mind accepts what is impressed upon it and whatever the conscious mind believes. It does not reason things out as the conscious mind does, and it does not argue or question the conscious mind's choices or beliefs.

The subconscious mind is like a bed of fertile soil that accepts any kind of seed, good or bad. Thoughts are seeds and are very dynamic. Positive and empowering thoughts will germinate and develop positive thoughts in your subconscious mind; similarly, negative, destructive seeds of thought grow negative thoughts in your subconscious mind. Every seed of thought, choices, and beliefs planted by the conscious mind on the subconscious mind will evidently emerge and take shape as an outer experience, accordingly, and in correspondence to their content.

Because all things are necessary to man's complete unfoldment, all things in human life are the work of God.

—WALLACE D. WATTLES

The subconscious mind does not care and does not engage in proving whether the thoughts are good or bad, true or false. It responds per the nature of your thoughts or submissions. For instance, if in your conscious mind, you assume or believe something to be true, even though it may be false, your subconscious mind will accept it as true and proceed to bring about results that must essentially follow because you consciously assumed and believed it to be true.

> Greatness is attained only by the thinking of great thoughts.
>
> —Wallace D. Wattles

The difference between the two varied functions of the one mind is that your conscious mind is the reasoning, objective, dynamic, and outer mind that makes all the physical choices based on the five senses. Your subconscious mind is the nonreasoning, subjective, passive, neutral, impartial, impersonal, nonselective, inner mind that accepts as true whatever your conscious mind believes to be true. Hence the importance of choosing positive and loving thoughts, ideas, and premises that empower, bless, and enrich you, and heal, inspire, and fill your soul, blissfully!

> You are not mentally developed by what you read, but by what you think about what you read.
>
> —Wallace D. Wattles

SIXTH SENSE

The conscious mind is often referred to as the objective mind because it deals with outward objects. The conscious mind or objective mind is limited to the objective world. Its medium of observation and collection of data, information, and experiences are within the limits of the five physical senses: what it can hear, see, smell, taste, and touch. The conscious or objective mind is the controller, navigator, captain, director, and frontal leader in the physical environment. It gathers information, knowledge, and experiences through the five sensory factors. The conscious mind or objective mind learns through observation, experience, and education. Reasoning and making choices are the greatest attributes and roles of the conscious (objective) mind.

The subconscious mind is the core of your being. It is infinite and pure energy. It is the spiritual entity, soul, and all-powerful and positive universal-love-energy and atom of God. It is the storehouse of infinite possibilities. It is the omnipotent and omnipresent sixth sense. That is why I chose to elevate and refer this all-powerful, inner-mind, spiritual energy, soul, and particle of God as the infinite Super-divine-subconscious mind, the sixth sense!

Though, often referred to as the subjective mind, your infinite Super-divine-subconscious (subjective) mind is aware of its environment—not by direct physical senses but by spiritual and intuitive means. Your subconscious (subjective) is the seat of your emotions and the storehouse of your memory. Your Super-divine-subconscious (subjective) mind performs its highest functions when your objective senses are not functioning. In other words, it is that intelligence that makes itself known when the objective mind is suspended or in a sleepy, drowsy state.

> Magic is believing in yourself; if you can do that, you can make anything happen.
>
> —Johann Wolfgang von Goethe

Your Super-divine-subconscious (subjective) mind sees without the use of the natural organs of vision. It has the capacity of clairvoyance and clairaudience—it possesses the infinite capacity to be in several places at a time. It can see and perceive events that are taking place elsewhere. It is the storehouse and realm of miracles and magic. Your Super-divine-subconscious (subjective) mind can leave your body, travel to distant lands, and gather useful information that is often of the most specific, exact, truthful, and real in appeal. Some spiritual and religious sects refer to this astonishingly powerful function of the infinite Super-divine-subconscious mind as *soul travel*. Through the infinite powers of the Super-divine-subconscious (subjective) mind, you can zero in on, connect to, and read the thoughts of others. Most successful people and great leaders of all ages have harnessed and applied the intuitive powers of their infinite Super-divine-subconscious minds, sixth sense, positively, to achieve rapport and build great and enriching relationships.

SIXTH SENSE

The human mind will not be confined to any limits.

—Johann Wolfgang von Goethe

When you understand the infinite powers of your Super-divine-subconscious mind, you can create and build a strong, rock-solid, and impenetrable aura, an empowering and protective positive energy wall around you and your loved ones.

Now that you understand the infinite powers of your Super-divine-subconscious mind, go ahead and put it to great use, positively! The infinite intelligence of your Super-divine-subconscious mind knows the answer to all your situations. It knows all things and will reveal the perfect answers to your innermost needs and desires.

Remember, your Super-divine-subconscious mind does not argue or dispute what it is told. You must be very careful to give your subconscious only those suggestions that heal, bless, elevate, and inspire you. Your subconscious mind doesn't understand a joke. It takes you at your word. If you give it the wrong information, it will accept it as true. It will then work to make that information correct. It will bring your suggestions, even those that were false, to pass as conditions, experiences, and events.

Your subconscious mind is the root of your habits. Everything that has happened to you happened because of thoughts impressed on your subconscious mind through perception and belief. If you have communicated wrong or distorted perceptions to your subconscious mind in the past, it is of vital importance to correct them. The definite and best way to do this is to repeatedly feed and enrich your subconscious mind with positive and stimulating thoughts. As you frequently and repeatedly plant such productive and useful thoughts to your Super-divine-subconscious mind, it accepts, believes, and makes them your habit. In this way, you can form new, healthier habits.

The habitual thinking of your conscious mind created the deep and strong roots in your subconscious mind. If your habitual thoughts are harmonious, peaceful, and positive, your subconscious mind will respond by creating harmony, peace, and productive conditions in your life.

> Go to your bosom: knock there and ask your heart what it doth know.
>
> —WILLIAM SHAKESPEARE

You can now harness and apply the affirmation tools in this book to reprogram and empower your subconscious mind to banish fear, superstitious beliefs, doubts, worry, stress, anger, hate, narrow-mindedness, and other limiting and destructive beliefs. The infinite powers of your Super-divine-subconscious mind are the source of all powers and the most creative energy in the divine-universe, and if you harness and use its omnipotent and omnipresent powers, positively,

SIXTH SENSE

you will achieve self-awareness, self-belief, self-control and strength, enlightenment, self-awareness and mastery, psychological freedom, balance, equilibrium, calmness, and power, and above all, bliss.

Your subconscious mind is susceptible and very sensitive to suggestions; because of that, your conscious mind serves as the gatekeeper, and one of its most crucial functions is to protect your subconscious mind from false impressions.

Your subconscious mind does not make comparisons or contrasts. It doesn't reason and think things out for itself. This latter function belongs to your conscious mind. Your subconscious mind simply reacts to the impressions given to it by your conscious mind. It does not pick and choose among different courses of action. It merely takes what it is given.

EUGENE N. NWOSU

For a man to achieve all that is demanded of him he must regard himself as greater than he is.

—Johann Wolfgang von Goethe

THE POWER OF AUTOSUGGESTION

Imagination is the beginning of creation. You imagine what you desire, you will what you imagine, and at last you create what you will.

—GEORGE BERNARD SHAW

AUTOSUGGESTION OCCURS WHEN you consciously suggest something definite and specific to your subconscious mind. Like any tool wrongly used, it can cause harm, but when used properly, it can be extremely helpful to banish fear, doubt, and other limiting and disempowering beliefs.

Suggestion is an enormously powerful force. Suggestion is the act or instance of putting something into one's mind. It is the mental process by which the thought or idea that has been suggested is entertained, accepted, or put into effect. Remember, a suggestion cannot impose itself on the subconscious mind against the will of the conscious mind. The conscious mind has the power to reject the suggestion.

Everyone has her or his own inner doubts, fears, feelings, and beliefs. These inner and traditional sentiments form the core of our choices and often go a long way to regulate and direct our lives.

A suggestion has no direct and holding power in and of itself. The power of any suggestion would take effect only if your conscious mind accepts it. The infinite powers of your Super-divine-subconscious mind will act and respond per whatever was accepted by your conscious mind.

Here are some money-related questions you can repetitively practice to empower and elicit constructive and productive responses from your Super-divine-subconscious mind:

- How can I add value to the lives of others and most easily make money?
- What will people pay for that I can easily and happily provide them with?
- What are the ways I can most easily and enjoyably reach financial freedom?
- What would I love to create that people would love to give me money for?

THE OUTSIDE FORCES

> When you permit an outside agency to control your feelings and emotions at frequent intervals for a prolonged period, your system will soon get into the habit of submitting to the control of this outside agency and will not respond any longer to any effort that the will may make to regain its original power of control.
>
> —CHRISTIAN D. LARSON

THROUGH ALL AGES and in every part of the world, the power of suggestion and propaganda has played a dominant part in the life and thought of humankind. Suggestion and propaganda have been used as a control mechanism by religious orders, political associations, cultural groups, traditional creeds, and corporate organizations to manipulate, flourish, and perpetuate themselves.

True religion is real living; living with all one's soul, with all one's goodness and righteousness.

—Albert Einstein

SIXTH SENSE

> The teaching of Jesus, if properly understood, would do away with organized temple worship altogether.
>
> —WALLACE D. WATTLES

Suggestions and propagandas can be used as a positive tool to influence good moral values and useful discipline in society. It can also be used to manipulate and take control and command over others who may not be familiar with how the conscious and subconscious mind works. When applied positively and constructively, they are very useful and magnificent tools for empowerment, but when used negatively, they become the most damaging and disempowering force on the minds of people.

> Be yourself—not your idea of what you think somebody else's idea of yourself should be.
>
> —HENRY DAVID THOREAU

Right from the very moment we are born, we are bombarded with incredible and very disempowering suggestions, and without knowing how to counter them, we unconsciously accept and believe them and internalize them as habits, which turn out to become our experience and reality.

Here are some examples of such negative and disempowering suggestions:

You can't. You'll never amount to anything. You are stupid. It's not what you know, but who you know. You mustn't. You are too old. You're lazy. Why bother? It's no use. You just can't win. There's hunger everywhere. Everyone is suffering. Things are getting worse and worse. You can't trust anybody. Watch out, you'll catch a terrible disease. Life is an endless grind. Love is for the birds. You can't trust people of such and such race, tribe, color, religion, sexual orientation, gender, or nationality.

> If you leave the smallest corner of your head vacant for a moment, other people's opinions will rush in from all quarters.
>
> —George Bernard Shaw

By allowing this kind of negative and disempowering view, most of the time unconsciously accepting them, you unwittingly collaborate in bringing them to pass and make them your experience and reality. As a child, you would have been helpless as you were being regularly barraged with the suggestions of others who were important to you, such as your parents, older siblings, guardians, teachers, television, religious leaders, and lately, social media. You may not have known any better. As a child, the workings of the conscious and unconscious mind were just another mystery you would not even imagine or consider.

SIXTH SENSE

You are now an adult, so you surely ought to have the knowledge and awareness to be able to make better choices. You can harness and use the tools of positive autosuggestion to recondition your subconscious mind from most of your wrong impressions.

Positive autosuggestion can free you from the limiting and disempowering effect of the negative verbal conditioning that might have otherwise altered your life pattern, making the advancement of good habits difficult.

> Nature intends all men and women to be mental and spiritual giants, and does not intend that anyone should follow the will of another.
>
> —CHRISTIAN D. LARSON

Every one of us was affected by other people's suggestions in our childhoods, in our teens, and in our adulthoods. If you look back, you can easily recall how parents, friends, relatives, teachers, and associates contributed to a campaign of negative suggestions. Study the things said to you, closely examine their underlying meanings, and you will discover that many of them were nothing more than a form of propaganda. The concealed purpose was—and is—to control you by instilling fear in you.

Subliminal autosuggestions go on in every home, school, office, factory, religious order, political association, organization, and club. You will find that many of the suggestions people make, whether they know it or not, are aimed at making you think, feel, and act as they want you to, in ways that are to their advantage, even if they are destructive to you.

The airwaves are full of subliminal autosuggestions. Every moment you turn on the radio or television, you are bombarded with news of calamity happening somewhere. The news is full of bad things that happened or are happening. When you are not being barraged with bad news, the advertisers are constantly pestering you with their products and services. The explosion of social media has virtually taken control of many people's conscious choices.

Every time you pick up the daily newspaper or turn on the television news, you hear several stories that could sow the seeds of futility, fear, worry, anxiety, and impending doom. These thoughts of fear can cause you to lose the will for life, if you accept them. Many of us have heard news stories and shivered a little at the thought that the world is full of mysterious and uncontrollable forces or that the world is about to end.

All the news stories, messages, and direct and subliminal suggestions of misfortune, sadness, and adversity have no power or influence over you and cannot hurt you. The only element that has any power or influence on you is the direction of your conscious mind. Uphold and affirm the positive to rekindle and validate the good in you, and you will banish any undesirable influence from outside forces.

Many are unaware that everything in the infinite universe is composed of positive-love-energy and is all connected. Yes, the world is full of forces—infinite, divine, omnipotent, and omnipresent, love-God's energy, which are neither mysterious nor uncontrollable.

Regularly pay attention to the information and suggestions that people make to you. You do not have to be at the mercy of anyone's controlling and destructive suggestion or influence. Break away from other people's overbearing influence.

> The true purpose of the strong is to promote greater strength in the weak, and not to keep the weak in that state where they are at the mercy of the strong.
>
> —Christian D. Larson

Stop allowing other people to do your thinking for you. Start now to choose your thoughts; make your own decisions and choices from an enlightened perspective and based on the everlasting realities and ethics of life and not from the viewpoint of ignorance, superstition, bigotry, and fear.

EUGENE N. NWOSU

> Prejudice is a burden that confuses the past,
> threatens the future, and renders the present
> inaccessible.
>
> —Maya Angelou

Ideas, information, and suggestions from others can affect you only if your conscious thought is in alignment with theirs. In other words, other people's ideas and suggestions have no direct power over you without your mental consent. You must entertain similar thoughts for them to get through to your subconscious mind. When you accept, and believe such information, ideas, or suggestions, it becomes your own thought, and the infinite powers of your Super-divine-subconscious mind receive such as truth and go to work to make certain that it delivers; the outcome or manifestation, in turn, becomes your experience and reality. But once you understand that you do not have to accept them, choices open for you. You can counteract such unhelpful ideas by consciously giving your subconscious mind positive and productive autosuggestions.

SIXTH SENSE

The way to control circumstances is to control the forces within yourself to make a greater man of yourself, and as you become greater and more competent, you will naturally gravitate into better circumstances. In this connection, we should remember that like attracts like. If you want that which is better, make yourself better. If you want to realize the ideal, make yourself more ideal. If you want better friends, make yourself a better friend. If you want to associate with people of worth, make yourself more worthy. If you want to meet that which is agreeable, make yourself more agreeable. If you want to enter conditions and circumstances that are more pleasing, make yourself more pleasing. In brief, whatever you want, produce that something in yourself, and you will positively gravitate towards the corresponding conditions in the external world.

—Christian D. Larson

DAILY AFFIRMATION TO EMPOWER THE SUBCONSCIOUS MIND

Any thought that is passed on to the subconscious often enough and convincingly enough is finally accepted.

—ROBERT COLLIER

YOU NOW HAVE the awareness and empowerment to choose the information, messages, and ideas that will uplift and enliven you. Choose joy and happiness! Choose vibrant health! Choose right action --- positive action (to do good)! Choose love and goodwill to all! Choose peace! Remember, you are love, I am love, we are love, we are soul, we are atom of God, and God is love in all essence.

For one swallow, does not make a summer, nor does one day; and so too one day, or a short time, does not make a man blessed and happy.

—ARISTOTLE

SIXTH SENSE

Go ahead and memorize the simple affirmations offered in this book, repeat the same to yourself regularly, several times a day, during your daily activities. I urge you to consciously and deliberately plant these very empowering seeds in the garden of your infinite Super-divine-subconscious mind to smoothen and transform your daily life, positively.

Always start your affirmations with the expression of gratitude, joy and happiness, fulfillment, and excitement. Your subconscious will mimic and believe the information your conscious mind suggests to it; you might as well give your subconscious mind the best of your vision and expectation. Whatever major premise your conscious mind assumes to be true, that determines the conclusion your subconscious mind will come to, no matter what the question or problem might be. If your premises are true, the conclusion must be true.

> One comes to believe whatever one repeats to oneself sufficiently often, whether the statement be true or false. It comes to be dominating thought in one's mind.
>
> —ROBERT COLLIER

Remember, your subconscious mind is infinite and all powerful yet neutral and impartial, and if you give it your highest vision and grand desires, it has the infinite capacity to make them happen for you. Conversely, if you pass on to it your doubts and fears, it will deliver the same without question.

> The more you think of what is right, the more you tend to make every action in your mind right. The more you think of the goal you have in view, the more life and power you will call into action in working for that goal. The more you think of your ambition, the more power you will give to those faculties that can make your ambitions come true. The more you think of harmony, of health, of success, of happiness, of things that are desirable, of things that are beautiful, of things that have true worth, the more the mind will tend to build all those things in yourself, provided, of course, that all such thinking is subjective.
>
> —CHRISTIAN D. LARSON

To change your life for greater good, you must design and equip your subconscious mind with positive and empowering seeds. The infinite intelligence of your Super-divine-subconscious mind will be accordingly and appropriately guided and directed to provide you with all the health, wealth, and prosperity for your spiritual, mental, and physical well being.

The affirmation formulas offered in this book may seem simplistic, but I guarantee that if you approach them with an open mind and practice them with faith and belief, they have the capacity to transform your entire existence beyond measure.

Commit the following affirmation to memory and repeat to yourself every time, every day, and always, positively!

> I am ever so very grateful. I am ever so very happy. I am ever so much fulfilled. I am ever so excited now that I truly and deeply know and strongly believe that in my own Infinite-divine-Universe, I choose joy and happiness today. I choose success today. I choose right action today. I choose love and goodwill to all today. I choose peace today. Because I am in conscious unity with that within me that is the Infinite-divine highest, I will obey my soul and be true to that within me that is the Infinite-divine highest. I am the supreme master of my Super-divine-subconscious mind. I am, God is, we are one!

You've always had the power to choose. Within the five sensory patterns, you have the capacity and freedom to choose positive, constructive, and productive thoughts. So, go on—choose joy and happiness! Choose success, wealth, prosperity, and abundance! Choose excellent and vibrant health! Choose a healthy, active, dynamic, and enriching lifestyle! Choose right actions! Choose love and goodwill to all! Choose peace! Choose to believe that something good will happen and is happening now! Choose to believe that you are truly worthy of all the good you desire!

The source and center of all man's creative power…is his power of making images, or the power of imagination.

—Robert Collier

Your subconscious is soul, spirit, pure energy, and atom of the omnipotent and omnipresent love-God; therefore, your subconscious is love. Your true self, that infinite "I," is basically a spirit in a human body that never dies. You have the infinite capacity to choose how and what your life becomes. Validate your greatness! Choose greatness! See the bigger picture! Choose bigger and worthy causes! Choose higher virtues!

The infinite intelligence of your Super-divine-subconscious mind has the limitless, omnipotent, and omnipresent power to make all your dreams come true accordingly and appropriately!

SIXTH SENSE

> Make every thought, every fact, that comes into your mind pay you a profit. Make it work and produce for you. Think of things not as they are but as they might be. Don't merely dream—but create!
>
> —Robert Collier

THINK GOOD THOUGHTS AND TRUST YOUR SUBCONSCIOUS MIND

> Use the imagination to picture only what is good, what is beautiful, what is beneficial, what is ideal, and what you wish to realize. Mentally see yourself receiving what you deeply desire to receive. What you imagine, you will think, and what you think, you will become. Therefore, if you imagine only those things that are in harmony with what you wish to obtain or achieve, all your thinking will soon tend to produce what you want to attain or achieve.
>
> —Christian D. Larson

Though your Super-divine-subconscious mind is all knowing and all wise, omnipotent, omnipresent, and omniscient, it does not argue with you or question any of your conscious decisions. So, when you harbor and express negative thoughts such as doubts, fears, and feelings of inadequacy, you will subsequently be impregnating your subconscious with these thoughts, and it will go to work, without hesitation, to make your doubts, fears, and limiting beliefs come true.

SIXTH SENSE

> We are always imagining something; it is practically impossible to be awake without imagining something. Then why not imagine something at, all times that will inspire the powers within us to do greater and greater things?
>
> —Christian D. Larson

Whatever your conscious mind decrees, your subconscious mind will accept without hesitation. If you give your subconscious mind the impression that you can't afford something or that you're not able to do something, it will do everything to make such a situation possible for you. Your subconscious does not know whether you were joking or whether you didn't mean what you were thinking at the time. Either way, your subconscious does not care. Its neutrality and impartiality is divine and pure. It is infinite, divine, love-energy, and will give you whatever you desire, good or bad, equally, without hesitation.

> Make the pattern clear, and make it beautiful; do not be afraid—make it grand. Remember that no limitation can be placed upon you by anyone but yourself; you are not limited as to cost or material; draw on the Infinite for your supply, construct it in your imagination; it must be there before it will ever appear anywhere else.
>
> —Charles Francis Haanel

Begin now to send the right commands to your subconscious. Whatever is your heart's desire, affirm and decree that you will have it. Believe and accept in your mind that it will be yours. Your infinite Super-divine-subconscious mind will collaborate, without hesitation or judgment, to bring your desires to fruition.

It doesn't matter how big the need. Nothing, absolutely nothing, is ever big enough for the infinite powers of your Super-divine-subconscious mind. It makes your wishes come true accordingly and at the most appropriate time, one way or another. Always give strong and positive signals to your subconscious mind. Assert to yourself that you truly and deeply know and strongly believe now that you can do all things through the infinite intelligence of your Super-divine-subconscious mind. Affirm and decree the following now to your subconscious mind in the present tense: "I truly and deeply know and strongly believe that in my own Infinite-divine-Universe, I can do all things through the infinite intelligence of my Super-divine-subconscious mind because I am, God is, we are one!"

There's a simple golden rule of the Infinite-divine-Universe that is common to all, which transcends all religious, spiritual, imaginable and unimaginable belief, which is good follows good and evil follows evil! If you have virtuous and worthy tendencies, worthy things will manifest in your life.

SIXTH SENSE

> What you admire in others will develop in yourself. Therefore, to love the ordinary in anyone is to become ordinary, while to love the noble and the lofty in all minds is to grow into the likeness of that which is noble and lofty.
>
> —CHRISTIAN D. LARSON

Remember, you are what you think all day long. If your conscious mind leans more on malicious and unworthy ideals, your subconscious will collaborate to bring about evil and distressing situations in your life. If you dwell more on good things, good things will follow, and if your conscious mind dwells more on evil things, evil things will follow.

You are not evil. No one is evil. No one was born evil. You are soul. Soul is pure, infinite, spirit, positive, love, and God's energy. We (you, me, and every humankind) are spirit in human body. Your mind is not evil. No force of nature is evil. It depends on how you apply the powers of divine-nature. Harness and use the infinite power of your conscious and subconscious mind, positively, to extend love and goodwill, blessings and joy, and inspiration and healing to all in the world.

> When you see evil, do not form ideas that
> are in the likeness of that evil; do not think
> of the evil as bad, but try to understand the
> forces that are back of that evil—forces that
> are good in themselves, though misdirected
> in their present state. By trying to understand
> the nature of the power that is back of evil
> or adversity, you will not form bad ideas,
> and therefore will feel no bad effects from
> experiences that may seem undesirable. At the
> same time, you will think your own thought
> about the experiences, thereby developing the
> power of the master mind.
>
> —Christian D. Larson

If you want the infinite powers of your Super-divine-subconscious mind to work for you constructively, you must give it the right request and you can be sure to get its cooperation, positively! It is always working for you. It is controlling your heartbeat, breath, and every fiber and organ in your body, this minute. When you cut your finger, it sets in motion the complex process of healing it. Its most fundamental tendency is lifeward. It is forever seeking to take care of you and preserve you.

So, when you set up obstacles, impediments, and delays in your conscious mind, you are denying the wisdom and intelligence resident in your infinite and Super-divine-subconscious mind. You are saying in effect that your subconscious mind cannot solve your problem. This leads to mental and emotional distress, illness, and depression.

Here's another affirmation formula to assist you to realize more of your desires; boldly affirm to yourself the following several times a day.

I am love. I am responsible. I am accountable. I am powerful. I am a winner. I am winning. I am financially independent. I am financially free. I am financially successful. I truly and deeply know and strongly believe that in my own Infinite-divine-Universe, I am one with the infinite intelligence of my Super-divine-subconscious mind, which knows no obstacles, difficulty, or delay.

I live in the joyous expectancy of the best. My deeper mind responds to my thoughts. I know that the work of the infinite power of my Super-divine-subconscious mind cannot be hindered. Infinite intelligence always finishes successfully whatever it begins.

Creative wisdom works through me, bringing all my plans and purposes to completion. Whatever I start, I bring to a successful conclusion.

My aim in life is to give wonderful service, and all those whom I contact are blessed by what I have, to offer. All my work comes to full fruition in divine order because I am in conscious unity with that within me that is the Infinite-divine highest. I will obey my soul and be true to that within me that is the Infinite-divine highest because I am the supreme master of my Super-divine-subconscious mind. I am, God is, we are one!

Evidently, your subconscious mind is equipped with infinite powers to flourish and act on its own if need be, yet it accepts the thought forms and imagery from your conscious mind. When you look for the answer to a problem, your subconscious will respond, but it expects you to come to a decision and true judgment in your conscious mind. You must acknowledge that the answer is in your subconscious mind.

You now have the enlightened awareness to know that whatever your conscious mind accepts and believes to be true, your subconscious mind will also assume and adopt as true. So, believe in the infinite intelligence of your Super-divine-subconscious mind for all the success and good fortune you desire, believe in love and goodwill to all, in right action, and in peace, joy, and happiness, and so it shall be for you, positively!

SIXTH SENSE

Thoughts are causes and conditions are effects. Herein is the explanation of the origin of both good and evil. Thought is creative and will automatically correlate with its object. This is a Cosmological Law, the Law of Attraction, the Law of Cause and Effect; the recognition and application of this law will determine both beginning and end; it is the law by which in all ages and in all times the people were led to believe in the power of prayer. "As thy faith is, so be it unto thee" is simply another, a shorter, and a better way of stating it.

—CHARLES FRANCIS HAANEL

THE MIGHTIEST POWER IN EXISTENCE

I am love! I am, God is, we are one!

THE QUOTE ABOVE is the scientific prayer that will enable you to get yourself or anyone else out of any difficulty. "I am love! I am, God is, we are one!" is the magic key—the secret to harmony, happiness, balance, equilibrium, and equanimity!

To those who have no acquaintance with the mightiest power in existence, this may appear to be a rash claim, but it needs only a fair trial to prove that, without a shadow of doubt, it is a just one. You need take no one's word for it, and you should not. Simply try it for yourself.

God is omnipotent, omnipresent, and omniscient, and we are God's image and likeness and have dominion over all things. This is the inspired teaching, and it is intended to be taken literally, at its face value. The ability to draw on this power is not the special prerogative of the mystic or the saint, as is so often supposed, or even of the highly-trained practitioner. Everyone has this ability whoever you are, wherever you may be; the golden key to harmony and abundance is in your hand now. This is because in scientific prayer, it is the infinite intelligence of your subconscious, the atom of God's love in you that does the work, and not you or your conscious self. So, your conscious limitations or weaknesses are of no account in the process. You are only the channel through which the divine action takes place.

Beginners often get startling results the first time, but all that is essential is to have an open mind and sufficient faith to try the experiment, regardless of your religious views or affiliations.

As for the actual method of working, like all fundamental things, it is simplicity itself. All you must do is this: stop thinking about the difficulty, whatever it is, and think about God's love instead. This is the complete rule, and if you do only this, the trouble, whatever it is, will disappear. It makes no difference what kind of trouble it is. It may be a big thing or a little thing; it may concern health, finances, a lawsuit, a quarrel, an accident, or anything else conceivable. Whatever it is, stop thinking about it and think of God's love instead—and repeat to yourself: "I am love! I am, God is, we are one"—that is all you must do.

It could not be simpler, could it? God could scarcely have made it simpler, and yet it never fails to work when given a fair trial.

Do not try to form a picture of God, which is impossible. Work by rehearsing: "I am love! I am, God is, we are one," or everything that you know about God. God is wisdom, truth, and inconceivable love. God is present in everything and everywhere, has infinite power, and knows everything. It matters not how well you may think you understand these things—go over them repeatedly.

> Do every common act as a god should do it;
> speak every word as a god should speak it.
>
> —WALLACE D. WATTLES

You must stop thinking of the trouble, whatever it is. The rule is to think about God. If you are thinking about your difficulty, you are not thinking about God. To be continually glancing over your shoulder to see how matters are progressing is fatal because it is thinking of the trouble, and you must think of God and nothing else. Your objective is to drive the thought of the difficulty out of your consciousness, for a few moments at least, substituting the thought of God. This is the crux of the whole thing. If you can become so absorbed in this consideration of the spiritual world that you forget for a while about the difficulty, you will find that you are safely and comfortably out of your difficulty—that your demonstration is made.

To apply the "I am love! I am, God is, we are one" magic key in difficult situations or to deal with a troublesome person, just repeat the phrase several times over, silently or aloud, then proceed to drive out all thought of the individual or the danger, replacing it with the thought of God.

SIXTH SENSE

By working in this way about a person, you are not seeking to influence the person's conduct in any way, except that you prevent him or her from injuring or annoying you, and you do the person nothing but good. Thereafter, he or she is certain to be in some degree a better, wiser, and more spiritual person. A pending lawsuit or other difficulty would probably fade out harmlessly without coming to a crisis, justice being done to all parties concerned.

If you find that you can do this very quickly, you may repeat the operation several times a day with intervals between. Be sure, however, that each time you do it, you drop all thought of the matter until the next time. This is important.

I have said that "I am love! I am, God is, we are one!" is simple, and so it is, but of course it is not always easy to believe and trust your God-self being your Super-divine-sub-consciousness. If you are very frightened or worried, at first it may be difficult to get your thoughts away from material things. But by constantly repeating a statement of absolute truth, you will soon find that the situation has begun to resolve and that your mind is clearing. These statements of truth can include "there is no power but God. I am the child of God, filled and surrounded by the perfect peace of God. God is love. God is guiding me now. God is with me." However mechanical or trite it may seem, do not struggle violently; be quiet but insistent. Each time you find your attention wandering, switch it back to: "I am love! I am, God is, we are one!"

Do not try to think in advance what the solution to your difficulty will be. This is called *outlining* and will only delay the process. Leave the question of ways and means to God. You want to get out of your difficulty sufficiently. You do your half, and God will never fail to do God's.

SIXTH SENSE

Whoever calls on the name of the Lord shall be saved.

—Acts 2:21 (NKJV)

SOME GUIDING PRINCIPLES FOR BALANCE, EQUILIBRIUM, AND EQUANIMITY

There is no harm in repeating a good thing.

—Plato

- Always look for the best in each person, situation, and thing.
- Resolutely turn your back on the past, good or bad, and live only in the present. Look forward to a better future.
- Forgive everybody without exception, and then forgive yourself wholeheartedly.
- Regard your job as sacred, and do your day's work to the best of your ability (whether you like it or not).
- Take every means to demonstrate healthy body and harmonious surroundings for yourself.
- Endeavour to make your life as much about service to others as possible, without interfering or fussing.
- Take every opportunity to share and spread your knowledge and wisdom, truthfully, to others.

SIXTH SENSE

- Rigidly refrain from personal criticism, and neither speak nor listen to gossip.
- Devote at least a quarter of an hour a day to affirmation, prayer, meditation, or contemplation.
- Read at least three pages of an inspirational, motivational, or spiritual book or article every day.
- Make it your prerogative to specifically claim spiritual understanding of yourself every day through affirmation, meditation, visualization, and/or spiritual prayers.
- Train yourself to give the first thought on waking to gratitude to God, and enliven your day with the magic key, silently or aloud, by reciting the following: "I am love! I am responsible! I am accountable! I am powerful! I am a winner! I am winning! Because I am, God is, we are one!"
- Practice the golden rule, which transcends all philosophies, spiritualities, and all religions: "Do unto others as they would to you." As Jesus said in the Bible, "Whatsoever ye would that men should do to you, do ye even so to them." The important point about the golden rule is that you are to practice it whether the other fellow does so or not.
- Above all, understand that whatever you see is but a picture that can be changed for the better by affirmation and strong belief.
- Ask yourself once a week how you are observing these timeless, age-old, divine principles.

THE AWAKENED AND EMPOWERED PRESENT!

> Our destiny is not mapped out for us by some exterior power; we map it out for ourselves. What we think and do in the present determines what shall happen to us in the future.
>
> —Christian D. Larson

LET THE INFINITE intelligence of your Super-divine-subconscious mind be open for abundance and joy in your life. You are destined for abundance and prosperity. You are surrounded by abundance. Your life is full of abundance. Empower and enliven your subconscious mind to claim your share of the immeasurable abundance.

The infinite intelligence of your Super-divine-subconscious mind will always have what you need, when you need it. The infinite universe is filled with abundance of resources for your health, wealth, joy, and happiness.

SIXTH SENSE

Man, alone, has the power to transform his thoughts into physical reality; man, alone, can dream and make his dreams come true.

—Napoleon Hill

Your life is yours to create. If you feed your subconscious mind with positive, constructive, and productive nourishments, you will have more than you ever dreamed possible. Infinite intelligence of your Super-divine-subconscious mind will see to it that money, wealth, and prosperity will flow in and through you in multiple streams, in avalanches of abundance, freely, copiously, and endlessly.

> Your opinion of your mental capacity may be great, but if your idea of intelligence is crude, your intelligence-producing thought will also be crude, and can produce only crude intelligence. It is therefore evident that to simply think that you are brilliant will not produce brilliancy, unless your understanding of brilliancy is made larger, higher and finer… When your thinking is brilliant, you will be brilliant, but if your thinking is not brilliant you will not be brilliant, no matter how brilliant you may think you are.
>
> —CHRISTIAN D. LARSON

Begin now to picture infinite abundance for yourself and others. Remember, there is more than enough of everything in the Infinite-divine-Universe for everyone. Everything in the universe is energy, including all the riches, wealth, and abundance. You are energy and part of all energy. All you need to do is desire, believe, and attract.

SIXTH SENSE

Everything you need to survive is all around you. You are surrounded by all the resources you need to live a healthy, wealthy, creative, joyful, prosperous, and peaceful life. You are surrounded by people who would be eager to contribute to your abundance. By constantly affirming the positive and appreciating the good in you and all that you have, you will manifest more abundance.

Your positive and prosperous thoughts will create your prosperous and abundant world. All you must do is connect to the source, being the infinite intelligence of your Super-divine-subconscious mind, send specific and clear commands of your desires, and abundance will come your way.

> Our success will not come from the acts of our forefathers, but can come alone from what we are doing now. Those who have inherited rich blood can use that richness in building greatness in themselves, but those who have not the privilege of such inheritance need not be discouraged. They can create their own rich blood and make it as rich as they like.
>
> —CHRISTIAN D. LARSON

You are born with the powers of miracles and magic. Remember, you are soul, infinite, and pure, and the core of your being is the omnipotent, omnipresent, and omniscient God's love and divine-energy. Therefore, you are surrounded with powers of miracle and magic everywhere you go. With the guidance of the omnipotent, omnipresent, and omniscient God's-love, your life will be filled with infinite wealth and abundance.

Wonderful things will happen to you if you live with the attitude of gratitude. Believe now that you are worthy of all that your heart desires. Invite and allow great and wonderful things to come into your life. And you will love the exciting opportunities and abundance that will come your way. You will live a life of passion, abundance, and success. You will joyfully acknowledge and appreciate all the blessings and abundance that become manifest in your life.

> All success in life, whether material or spiritual, starts with the thoughts that you put into your mind every second of every minute of every day. Your outer world reflects the state of your inner world. By controlling the thoughts that you think and the way you respond to the events of your life, you begin to control your destiny.
>
> —R. Sharma

You will produce financial abundance doing what you love; be grateful for every single moment in your life. You will be constantly presented with opportunities for success. Open your heart today to receive all the opportunities that surround you. Go now and manifest all the abundance you desire with the affirmation tools you have received from this book, including the following:

I am love. I am responsible. I am accountable. I am powerful. I am a winner. I am winning. I am financially independent. I am financially free. I am financially successful. I truly and deeply know and strongly believe that in my own Infinite-divine-Universe, I am one with the infinite intelligence of my Super-divine subconscious mind, which knows no obstacles, difficulty, or delay.

I live in the joyous expectancy of the best. My deeper mind responds to my thoughts. I know that the work of the infinite power of my Super-divine-subconscious mind cannot be hindered. Infinite intelligence always finishes successfully whatever it begins.

Creative wisdom works through me, bringing all my plans and purposes to completion. Whatever I start, I bring to a successful conclusion.

My aim in life is to give wonderful service, and all those whom I contact are blessed by what I have, to offer. All my work comes to full fruition in divine order because I am in conscious unity with that within me that is the Infinite-divine highest. I will obey my soul and be true to that within me that is the Infinite-divine highest because I am the supreme master of my Super-divine-subconscious mind. I am, God is, we are one!

AWAKEN YOUR OMNIPOTENT POWERS NOW!

> Whatever you habitually think yourself to be, that you are. You must form, now, a greater and better habit; you must form a conception of yourself as a being of limitless power, and habitually think that you are that being. It is the habitual, not the periodical, thought that decides your destiny.
>
> —Wallace D. Wattles

THE INFINITE POWER of your Super-divine-subconscious mind is astonishing and immeasurable. It is the source of all powers and the core of wisdom that connects you directly with the omnipotence and omnipresence. This is the power that moves the world, guides the planets in their course, causes the sun to shine and the moon to circle the planets, and sustains nature and humankind simultaneously.

It uplifts, stimulates, inspires, motivates, and directs your actions and protects you. It generates its infinite powers direct from the ocean of love and mercy, being the

SIXTH SENSE

universal love-energy, God. It has the powers of total recall from the experiences, scenes, and images of your memory's storehouse.

Your Super-divine-subconscious mind controls your heartbeat, organs, tissues, and the circulation of your blood. It regulates your digestion, assimilation, and elimination. When you eat a piece of any food, your Super-divine-subconscious mind transmutes it into tissue, muscle, bone, and blood.

Your Super-divine-subconscious mind knows the answers to all your problems. It controls all the vital processes and functions of your body. These extraordinary processes are far beyond any human comprehension.

Your Super-divine-subconscious mind is always on the job; it never sleeps and never rests. You can discover the miracle-working power of your Super-divine-subconscious mind by simply stating to your subconscious prior to sleep that you want a specific thing accomplished. You will be astounded and delighted to realize that forces within you will be released that lead to the result you wished for.

> First comes thought; then organization of that thought, into ideas and plans; then transformation of those plans into reality. The beginning, as you will observe, is in your imagination.
>
> —NAPOLEON HILL

Your Super-divine-subconscious mind is the source of all your creative and humane ideals, aspirations, and loving and altruistic motives. It was through the infinite intelligence of the Super-divine-subconscious mind that great artists, philosophers, and creative writers perceived and communicated great truths hidden from the average man of the day.

The infinite intelligence of your Super-divine-subconscious mind, your sixth sense, can give you independence of time and space. It can make you free of all pain and suffering. It can give you the answer to all problems, whatever they may be. Your sixth sense is a power and an intelligence within you that far transcends your intellect, causing you to marvel at the wonder of it all. When you awaken, and empower the infinite intelligence of your Super-divine-subconscious mind you will be excited and joyful at the miracle-working powers latent in your own subconscious mind.

SIXTH SENSE

Prosperity is a harmonious, creative state of being. Creative law will overcome every kind of disharmony, whether it be financial, physical, mental, moral, or social.

—CHARLES FRANCIS HAANEL

YOUR INSIDE-OUT "BOOK OF LIFE"

Man, is what he thinks all day long.

—RALPH WALDO EMERSON

WHATEVER YOU IMPRESS on your subconscious mind, through your conscious thoughts, you will experience as the objective manifestation of circumstances, conditions, events, and situations in your life. Whatever thoughts, beliefs, opinions, theories, or dogmas you inscribe, engrave, or impress on your subconscious mind, through your conscious thoughts, will manifest outward and become your reality. You will experience them as the objective manifestation of circumstances, conditions, and events. What you carve, draw, or paint on the inside you will experience on the outside. Remember, you have two sides to your life: objective and subjective, visible and invisible, thoughts and manifestations.

Dig within. Within is the wellspring of good; and it is always ready to bubble up, if you just dig.

—MARCUS AURELIUS

SIXTH SENSE

Your thoughts are received as a pattern of neural firings in your cerebral cortex, which is the organ of your conscious reasoning mind. Once your conscious or objective mind accepts the thought completely, it is transmitted to the other parts of the brain, where it becomes flesh and is made manifest in your experience.

As previously outlined, your subconscious cannot argue. It acts only from your conscious input. It accepts your judgment or the decisions of your conscious mind as final. Therefore, you are continually writing on your "book of life" because your thoughts become your experiences.

Society exists only as a mental concept; in the real world, there are only individuals.

—Oscar Wilde

The power to move the world is in the infinite intelligence of your Super-divine-subconscious mind, which has boundless wisdom. It generates its infinite powers directly from the omnipotent and omnipresent universal energy force, the source, the ocean of love and mercy, the core of all things, the law of life, and God's love. Whatever you impress upon the infinite intelligence of your Super-divine-subconscious mind, through your conscious thoughts, the latter will collaborate and move heaven and earth to bring it to pass. You must, therefore, impress it with positive, productive, useful ideas, and inspiring and motivating thoughts.

There is so much chaos and misery in the world because so many people are ignorant of the relationship and interface between their conscious and subconscious minds. When these two principles are in accord, in concord, in peace, and synchronously together, you will have health, happiness, peace, and joy. There is no sickness or discord when the conscious and subconscious work together harmoniously and peacefully.

> The universal order and the personal order are nothing but different expressions and manifestations of a common underlying principle.
>
> —MARCUS AURELIUS

There is an ancient story of Hermes Trismegistus that had the reputation of being the greatest, most powerful Magus (a member of a hereditary priestly class among the ancient Medes and Persians and one of the traditionally three wise men from the East paying homage to the infant Jesus) the world had ever known. When his tomb was opened centuries after his passing, those who were in touch with the wisdom of the ancients waited with great expectancy and a sense of wonder. It was said that the greatest secret of the ages would be found within the tomb. And so, it was. The secret was "as within, so without; as above, so below." In other words, whatever you impress in your subconscious mind becomes expressed on the screen of space. This same truth was pronounced by

SIXTH SENSE

Moses, Isaiah, Jesus, Buddha, Zoroaster, Laotze, and all the illumined seers of the ages. Whatever you feel as true subjectively is expressed as conditions, experiences, and events. Motion and emotion must balance. As in heaven (your own mind), so on earth (in your body and environment).

EUGENE N. NWOSU

Heaven is not a place or a condition. It is merely an awareness of perfect oneness.

—Helen Schucman

SIXTH SENSE

> It is clear, therefore, that thoughts of abundance will respond only to similar thoughts; the wealth of the individual is seen to be what he inherently is. Affluence within is found to be the secret of attraction for affluence without. The ability to produce is found to be the real source of wealth of the individual. It is for this reason that he who has his heart in his work is certain to meet with unbounded success. He will give and continually give, and the more he gives the more he will receive.
>
> —Charles Francis Haanel

You will find throughout all of nature the law of action and reaction, of rest and motion. These two must balance, and then there will be harmony and equilibrium. You are here to let the life principle flow through you rhythmically and harmoniously. The intake and the output must be equal. The impression and the expression must be equal. All your frustration is due to unfulfilled desires.

If you think negatively, destructively, and viciously, these thoughts generate destructive emotions that must be expressed and must find an outlet. These emotions, being of a negative nature, are frequently expressed as ulcers, heart trouble, tension, and anxieties.

> Achievement of any kind is the crown of effort, the diadem of thought. By the aid of self-control, resolution, purity, righteousness, and well-directed thought a man ascends. By the aid of animality, indolence, impurity, corruption, and confusion of thought a man descends.
>
> —JAMES ALLEN, *As a Man Thinketh*

What is your idea or feeling about yourself now? Every part of you expresses that idea. Your vitality, body, financial condition, friends, and social status represent a perfect reflection of the ideas you have of yourself. This is the real meaning of what is impressed in your subconscious mind and what is expressed in all phases of your life.

> Man, is made or unmade by himself; in the armoury of thought he forges the weapons by which he destroys himself; he also fashions the tools with which he builds for himself heavenly mansions of joy and strength and peace.
>
> —JAMES ALLEN, *As a Man Thinketh*

We injure ourselves by the negative ideas we entertain. How often have you wounded yourself by getting angry, fearful, jealous, or vengeful? These are the poisons that enter your subconscious mind. You were not born with these negative attitudes. Feed your subconscious mind life-giving thoughts, and you will wipe out all the negative patterns lodged within it. As you continue to do this, all the past will be wiped out and remembered no more.

Nothing appears on your body except when the mental equivalent is first in your mind. As you change your subconscious mind by drenching it with incessant affirmations, you replenish and transform your body.

EUGENE N. NWOSU

Treat those who are good with goodness, and treat those who are not good with goodness. Thus, goodness is attained. Be honest to those who are honest, and be also honest to those who are not honest. Thus, honesty is attained.

—Lao Tzu

YOUR SUBCONSCIOUS IS IN CONTROL ALWAYS!

Nothing can go wrong in this world but yourself; and you can go wrong only by getting into the wrong mental attitude.

—WALLACE D. WATTLES

WHETHER YOU ARE awake or asleep, the ceaseless, tireless action of your subconscious mind controls all the vital functions of your body without any need for your conscious mind to intervene. While you are asleep, your heart continues to beat rhythmically. Your chest and diaphragm muscles pump air in and out of your lungs. The carbon dioxide that is the byproduct of the activity of your body's cells is exchanged for the fresh oxygen you need to go on functioning. Your subconscious controls your digestive processes and glandular secretions, as well as all the other wondrously complex operations of your body. All this happens whether you are awake or asleep.

If you were forced to operate your body's functions with your conscious mind, you would certainly fail. You would probably die a very quick death. The processes are too complicated, too intertwined. The heart-lung machine that is used during open-heart surgery is one of the wonders of modern medical technology, but what it does is infinitely simpler than what your subconscious mind does twenty-four hours a day, year in and year out.

Suppose you were crossing the ocean in a supersonic jetliner and you wandered into the cockpit. You certainly would not know how to fly the plane, but you might distract the pilot and cause a problem. In the same way, your conscious mind cannot operate your body, but it can get in the way of proper functioning and operation of your subconscious mind.

> *There is no hurry. There is only God, and all is well with the world.*
>
> —WALLACE D. WATTLES

Worry, anxiety, fear, and depression interfere with the normal functioning of the heart, lungs, stomach, and intestines. The medical community is just beginning to appreciate how serious so-called stress-related diseases are. The reason is that these patterns of thought interfere with the harmonious functioning of your subconscious mind.

Whenever you dwell on obstacles, delays, and difficulties, the infinite intelligence of your Super-divine-subconscious mind responds accordingly, and you block your own good.

SIXTH SENSE

When you feel physically and mentally disturbed, the best thing you can do is to let go, relax, and still the wheels of your thought processes. Speak to the infinite intelligence of your Super-divine-subconscious mind. Tell it to take over in peace, harmony, and divine order. You will find that all the functions of your body will become normal again. Be sure to speak to your Super-divine-subconscious mind with authority and conviction. It will respond by carrying out your command.

WATCH YOUR THOUGHTS!

You can develop any power which is or has been shown by any person anywhere. Nothing that is possible in spirit is impossible in flesh and blood. Nothing that you can think is impossible. Nothing that you can imagine is impossible of realization.

—Eugene N. Nwosu

THE PRINCIPLE OF action and reaction is the natural and divine law of the infinite universe. Your thought is action, and the reaction is the automatic response of the infinite intelligence of your Super-divine-subconscious mind to your thought. Therefore, you should carefully watch all the ideas and thoughts you cultivate in your conscious mind and allow them to penetrate your subconscious mind.

What the creative principle of the infinite intelligence of your Super-divine-subconscious mind created, it can re-create. Per your belief, it will be done unto you!

SIXTH SENSE

> Nothing was ever in any man that is not in you; no man ever had more spiritual or mental power than you can attain, or did greater things than you can accomplish. You can become what you want to be.
>
> —Wallace D. Wattles

The first thing to realize is that your subconscious mind is always working. It is active night and day, whether you act upon it or not. Your subconscious is the builder of your body, but you cannot consciously perceive or hear that inner process. Your business is with your conscious mind and not your subconscious mind. Just keep your conscious mind busy with the expectation of the best, and make sure the thoughts you habitually think are based on things that are lovely, true, just, and harmonious. Begin now to take care of your conscious mind, knowing in your heart and soul that the infinite intelligence of your sixth sense, the Super-divine-subconscious mind, is always expressing, reproducing, and manifesting per your habitual thinking.

Before you go to sleep, turn over any request to the infinite intelligence of your sixth sense, the Super-divine-subconscious mind, and prove its miracle-working power to yourself. The Infinite-divine-Universal energy, ominipotent, ominipresent, omniscience subconscious love-energy, being the supreme God's love in all things will flow through you rhythmically and harmoniously if you consciously affirm the following:

> I truly and deeply know and strongly believe that in my own Infinite-divine-Universe, the infinite intelligence of my Super-divine-subconscious power that gave me this desire is now fulfilling it through me, because I am in conscious unity with that within me that is the infinite divine highest. I will obey my soul and be true to that within me that is the Infinite-divine highest because I am the supreme master of my Super-divine-subconscious mind. I am, God is, we are one!

Remember, the infinite intelligence of your Super-divine-subconscious mind controls all the vital processes of your body and knows the answer to all problems. Just as water takes the shape of the pipe it flows through, the life principle in you flows through you per the nature of your thoughts.

It is your infinite divine right to claim that the healing presence in your Super-divine-subconscious mind is flowing through you as harmony, health, peace, joy, and abundance. Think of it as a living intelligence and lovely companion along the way. Firmly believe it is continually flowing through you vivifying, inspiring, and prospering you. It will respond exactly this way. It will be done unto you as you believe!

SIXTH SENSE

You can do anything you think you can. This knowledge is literally the gift of the gods, for through it you can solve every human problem. It should make of you an incurable optimist. It is the open door.

—Robert Collier

Whatever you impress on the infinite intelligence of your sixth sense, the Super-divine-subconscious mind, is expressed on the screen of space as conditions, experiences, and events. You can hinder the normal rhythm of your heart, lungs, and other organs by worry, anxiety, and fear.

Empower your subconscious with harmonious, healthy, and peaceful thoughts, and all the functions of your body will become normal again. Keep your conscious mind busy with the expectation of the best, and the infinite intelligence of your sixth sense, the Super-divine-subconscious mind, will, in effect, reciprocate and faithfully reproduce your habitual thinking.

Envision the happy ending or solution to any challenging situation or problem; feel the excitement of triumph and accomplishment, and what you visualize and feel will be acknowledged by the infinite intelligence of your sixth sense, the Super-divine-subconscious mind, which will make it manifest.

EUGENE N. NWOSU

In dwelling, live close to the ground. In thinking, keep to the simple. In conflict, be fair and generous. In governing, don't try to control. In work, do what you enjoy. In family life, be completely present.

—Lao Tzu

EUGENE N. NWOSU

To be good is noble; but to show others how to be good is nobler.

—Mark Twain

He is the author of the best-selling book *Cut Your Own Firewood—the Ultimate Power to Succeed*, first published in 1998 by The Collins Press, Cork, Ireland; and by popular demand republished in 2006 by Amazon Books. He created the audio cassette program *The Ultimate Power to Succeed in the 21st Century* that focuses on entrepreneurial success and personal happiness. He is also the author of *Optimal Edge—Unlocking and Enhancing Leadership Potential and Excellence in People and Organisations.* His careers encompassed administration, management, accountancy, and holistic human development with more than thirty years of combined corporate and entrepreneurial wealth of experience. He is a human resource and learning and development professional, leadership success coach and mentor, executive life and business coach and mentor, and entrepreneur. His elemental purpose is helping people and organizations lead effectively and achieve success, peace, joy, and happiness, and a life of balance, equilibrium, and equanimity. He lives in Dublin, Ireland, sharing a joyful and experiential life of gratitude and love with his wife, three biological children, and foster children, which he embraces dearly as one of his most humbling and experientially fulfilling life journeys.

Made in the USA
Columbia, SC
18 June 2017